Walking on Air

Books by Pierre Delattre

Tales of a Dalai Lama

Walking on Air

Walking on Air

Pierre Delattre

Houghton Mifflin Company Boston 1980

Library of Congress Cataloging in Publication Data

Delattre, Pierre, date
    Walking on air.

    I. Title.
PZ4.D3395Wal [PS3554.E44]   813'.54   79-28637
ISBN 0-395-29118-6
ISBN 0-395-29119-4 pbk.

Printed in the United States of America

V 10 9 8 7 6 5 4 3 2 1

For Nancy Ortenstone
and
The Happiness Gorillas

O, the fabulous wings unused, folded in the heart.
— CHRISTOPHER FRY

Nothing happens! Or has everything happened,
and are we standing now, quietly, in the new life?
— JUAN RAMON JIMÉNEZ

Walking on Air

1 ✍

EVERYONE HERE IS UPSET because Boomie has taken another lover. Mamouli and Papouli say we have no choice but to find a role for him and include him in the circus. That won't be easy. We are a very small circus whose mystical purpose can be destroyed by the slightest loss of equilibrium. Our situation has been precarious enough since the Great Grand-Papouli died four years ago. But thanks to the audience, upon whose energy we have learned to rely in ever more subtle ways, we have survived without further loss to humans or animals. Twice we almost lost Boomie. Now for the third time Boomie has stayed in her wagon with a man and won't come out to perform. She took him into her wagon a week ago, and they've been there ever since. All of us at The Great Papouli Circus fear for what she will end up doing to herself if we don't handle this just right. We love her, of course, and we are also bound to her.

It is Boomie's vocation to be erotically exciting, and

nobody who sees her can fail to respond. But our circus family, as one body, is so tuned to her that she is literally the source of sexual generation among us. Without her, our performances lose the power to attract. The audiences lack attention. The stands are full of flurry and distraction. Arguments and fistfights erupt.

Boomie's aficionados, some of whom tracked us down from thousands of miles away, even from distant countries, are growing restless. I've done the best I can by building them a little campground with tents and privies and a canteen, but most of them are at the end of their patience. She can't stay in there forever, we tell them. Make her come out now, they say. Who's the boss around here, anyhow? Oh, no, say I, this is an entirely voluntary circus, it couldn't work any other way. Papouli isn't one of those ringmasters with a whip. The only one who uses a whip is Boomie, and that's only to pop the cigarette from my mouth or to snap the buttons off my pants when I'm playing the clown. Polyphemus carries a whip into the lions' cage, but that's as much for show as the cage is. Whatever Calypso and his pride do is of their own free will, just as it is with all of us.

So we go on performing for the small, disgruntled crowd, and we watch Boomie's wagon and wait. The birds perched on her roof are singing more cheerfully than ever. At least they're pleased by what's going on. Boomie's wagon is in its usual place, far from the others, in a corner of the field where we've encamped at the outskirts of town. It's an attractive wagon with red-spoked golden hubs, bright butterfly designs on both sides, shuttered windows and a silver stairway leading up to the door. Her flying motorcycle is parked in front. That's what she picked him up on. She was bringing up the rear of our caravan when she pulled over to the ditch to talk to a young man lying in the wildflowers against his pack. For several hours she wasn't with us, and Papouli was about to send someone to see if she was all right when she came roaring around the bend with the youth seated behind her, pressed against her back. I suppose they've been that close ever since.

Her shutters have been open at night. A constant flicker of candlelight glows. We've tried to get Polyphemus to kind of amble on over and have a peek inside, just to make sure Boomie's okay. Tall as he is, he could glance in the window. But, like every other giant I've known, he's too much the gentleman. Annie the Elephant only communicates with Mamouli, and whatever our circus mother knows she's keeping to herself; or perhaps she told Papouli, because he certainly doesn't seem worried for Boomie's immediate safety. He says we have to accept her as the difficult one of the family. Someone with so much sexual energy is bound to get into trouble now and then. Mamouli sees in Boomie's sporadic urges to mate an instinctual need not only to complete her own body but to complete the mystical body of our circus, whose connection to the cosmos has become so tenuous since the death of our patriarch. How many near calamities have occurred since then? Yet we've maintained the balance, haven't we? Though Boomie's choices of men thus far have been useless for the circus and disastrous for her, Mamouli says we should have compassion for her and not begrudge her the right to be sated by the lover of her choice, even if the repercussions terrify us and we don't know how to allay them.

Like the rest of us, Boomie has a number of acts. She

3

dives from on high into a four-foot tank of water. Impressive, but only a trick, seeing as how Jack and Jill, our performing dolphins, are waiting in the water to snatch her and whirl her around. Boomie's bird act is breathtakingly beautiful, especially in summer when many birds from the fields join the ones who travel with us. Boomie stands in the ring with arms outspread. From out of the night, pairs of birds swoop into the tent and settle upon her body, until she herself becomes a large bird entirely covered with feathers. It's my control of the spotlight that makes her seem to spread wings of her own and fly out of the tent. All she has to do is walk away quietly and climb into the glass dolphin tank. Jack and Jill hold her on the surface between them until later, when a light glows up through the water as she emerges magically from the deep and rides them round and round the rising vortex.

Boomie didn't train the dolphins. They trained her, with a little help from Mamouli. The birds conceived their giant bird stunt out of the sheer pleasure of flocking into the shape of her body. Their ease in carrying the eyes of the audience upward, as much as my control of the lights, accounts for the way she seems to vanish from the ground. Birds are so attracted to Boomie they don't need to be coaxed to join the act. Pairs of birds she has never met before sometimes flit in, local birds eager for a new diversion. Some only visit, others stay to become part of the regular troop. They train themselves, set up their own camps in the trees. The flock keeps growing. It flies above and about our caravan as we journey the backroads of the land. The birds swoop off across the fields, into the hills and back again, creating the most magnificent zooming, swirling patterns in the sky, before stopping to rest in the groves or on the wagon tops. We all love Boomie's birds, but they fly in of their own accord, out of desire, just as a man or a woman will occasionally walk down from the stands, almost in a trance, to kiss her body.

As far as her attraction goes, Boomie seems to have been born with it. Most of her tricks rely more upon image than discipline. Flying her motorcycle over barrels, snapping cigarettes from my mouth with her bullwhip, playing various sexy-lady parts on the spinning rope we call the web. But her main act has required a tremendous amount of training and has had to emerge from deep within her own character, as all great acts do. We are what you might call a circus people's circus. Professionals come from far and wide to observe what we do best; and certainly there are many who regard Boomie with the greatest reverence. Because of the danger she places herself in, and because of the particularly horrible destiny her tragic flaw has proclaimed as almost inevitable, she has become a kind of legend for others, and for us at times like this a source of anxiety bordering on hysteria.

I don't think anybody has slept since Boomie took that young man into her wagon. How will her passion for him affect her greatest act — the one she performs as Boomie the Boomerang Lady? For those of you who have never seen The Great Papouli Circus, let me describe it.

Boomie performs her finale in the nude, except, in recent years, for a pair of waterproof ruby-red patent leather boots she wears to disguise an artificial foot. Let me say that hers is not the tanned, full-fleshed body the rest of us possess. Her figure is slim, willowy, almost frail, her skin absolutely white, and the absence of a left arm below the elbow has somehow not only added to her vulnerability but has made her more stunningly attractive. Her flame-red hair falls to her knees, with aery strands that reflect glints of gold from the floodlights. Her bush is a nest of flame, set on a full mound below her long, flat belly. She enters the tent bareback, astride a white horse. They prance up to the Circle of the Moon.

Our circus has two rings: the larger Ring of the Sun with a bright red curb, at the center, and the smaller silver-rimmed Ring of the Moon to the north. Boomie slips off the horse, he trots away, and she stands against a board, the kind you may have seen a woman place herself in front of while a man throws knives at her. I arrive with the knives, but not to throw them. As far as I know, Boomie the Boomerang Lady is the only performer in the world who throws knives at *herself*.

The knives are bright blue crescent moons with silver blades along the entire curve of the outer edge. A wire net drops around the far south curve of the arena. I hand her one knife at a time and step back. She flings the boomerang. It swirls slowly and silently into the dark upper regions of the tent, then reappears, winging toward her, its blade flashing until, as she stands with arms outspread, it strikes home, stuck in the board, close to her body. Twelve blades I hand her. They strike to either side of her hips, her knees, her ankles, her chest, her neck. She steps out each time to throw, then steps back against the board. Next to last, the boomerang thunks deep into the wood just above her head. An inch lower and she would scalp herself. For the last throw she asks for a mirror, steps a few feet back, facing the board this time, and, looking into the mirror, throws the blade so that it flies upward to the north, circles south, drops low, swoops down the center and zings home between her legs.

That is when the crowd goes wild and the birds fly in.

2

THE BIG CIRCUSES keep their animals tied up or in cages at all times. The small, cozy ones like ours might pretend to, but of course we don't. They're our friends.

Our animals are perfectly free to wander about after the night crowd departs. Just so they don't stray too far. We only keep them in cages when the public's around, because of the law and because people would be frightened. Fright frightens animals.

Expect a good performance and you'll get it from a circus animal, but expect to be mauled or eaten alive and you'll get that too. Not that our animals behave like primitives. They're educated. But their eagerness to please is directed toward our fantasies. They go straight for the imagination. In a world where violent images fill the mind, one must exercise a bit of caution.

When we're on the road, we always take the opportunity to give them a romp in the woods or in a field, if there's nobody around to watch; and, as I say, the nights are theirs once the audience has gone home. But we have these pilgrims waiting to see Boomie. They're a strange lot — women in leather, men dressed like parrots or butterflies. An odor of perfume hovers over them. What would these exotics do if our lion, Calypso, and his pride of six scampered into their tents to lick up some of that scent from their necks and thighs? Even if we told them the animals were harmless, how would they take it if Annie's trunk poked into their pants to sniff around, or if Pegasus, who has been feeling left out since Boomie stopped riding him, came hindwalking into the light of their campfire, snorting and pawing and trying to convince them he was a flying horse? Fetch and his flock of poodles don't worry us too much, though he looks so much like a wolf and they so much like lambs that one can't utterly discount the possibility of another incident like the one last year, when the shepherd saw them in his field and put a load of buckshot into poor Fetch's rear. And of course there's Dad the Gorilla, as placid a character as ever thumped a chest, but not the kind a stranger would want to smoke a cigar with. When Dad smells a cigar he just hasn't gotten the hang of asking for one politely; and if it's Cuban he has a way of emptying your pockets fast: fun if you relax, yet a bit startling if you don't expect to be lifted up, flipped over, held by the ankles and shaken out. Mr. and Mrs. Solomon are the only ones nobody need worry about except me. (A clown can never entirely trust a chimp.) They've been stick-in-the-mud stay-at-homes ever since Papouli gave them their own wagon.

So, you see, the animals are accustomed to freedom, and they've been feeling insulted lately because we won't let them go out at night. They're punishing us by not performing well. Dad pretends he can't even bend a tire. There's nothing as depressing to watch as a pooped gorilla. The Solomons roller-skate and ride their bicycles perfectly, but without throwing the tantrum that's the whole point of their act. Rhumba, Bamba, Samba, Conga, Raspa and Cha-Cha (the lionesses) refused to dance for Polyphemus. He had to promise Calypso three days' worth of prime rib before the old lion would get them to line up and swing, which was not only extortion but also humiliated the giant whom everybody could plainly see was no lion tamer at all, merely a front man for the shaggy old beast who really controls the action in the cage.

Enough. I don't blame them. At least we let them horse around in the tent tonight until they were making such a racket with their whinnies, snarls, barks and grunts that Papouli had to tell them to shut up so we could have our powwow.

• •

We were seated in a circle on the curb of the Sun Ring, where Papouli had assembled us to discuss the situation. I don't know why Papouli bothers to ask our opinions, since his ideas are the only ones that count. I love the man as much as anyone else, but I'm not afraid to say there's a bit of fraud in his pretense at democracy.

Mamouli started out with her usual offer to save the show by dropping the tightrope for the final act and walking on air. Mamouli has long believed that she once walked on air and will do it again some day. According to her, the only reason she's failed so far is that Papouli won't let her perform without a net. One cannot walk on air, she insists, without the absolute faith of everyone present, performers and animals alike. A net would advertise our doubts. Papouli, with that evangelistic flair of his, could certainly stir up the faith of the audience if he had enough faith of his own to sustain him.

"Everybody in the family believes in me except you," she said. "Why can't you let go of your fear? Make the leap of faith. Your old Mamouli'll do the rest. If you wait much longer, you'll lose your chance to save this circus."

Papouli rolled his eyes. "Are you through?"

We all laughed, I'm ashamed to say. As Papouli goes, so go we. That's our weakness and our strength. Even Mamouli, whose laughter is helplessly triggered by the laughter of others — I never dare clown while she's performing lest the audience response make her giggle herself off balance — even Mamouli laughed, despite herself, and that kept Papouli going. Does he think she's really amused by his insults?

"You may be poetry in motion, sweetheart," — he winked at us — "but nothing you've shown me so far makes this old rope walker willing to suspend anything quite as frayed as his disbelief."

We really roared at that one, to show we caught on to his allusion, damn it. Why do we make fun of Mamouli? Which one of us hasn't secretly believed that some day he'll be able to walk on air? Mamouli has more nerve than we do, that's all. More of the ultimate spiritual chutzpah.

Nights when I stay up late to keep the books, I sometimes look out to the porch of the Papouli wagon and see her perched at the edge of the stoop in the moonlight,

11

crouched naked with her arms back, her breasts profiled like two great weights hung down to hold her earthward. Don't laugh, but I imagine air whistling out through the nipples as she lifts her swarthy shoulders, clenches her fists and walks up into the sky. She's never quite done it, but she will any time now.

I, Bob the Grip, predict it.

It's inspiring to look upon such singleness of purpose — the way she gets up on her toes and stays balanced there for the longest time. I can sometimes see the Solomons at their window watching her, too, while the late-late movie flickers behind them on the TV and they claw excitedly at one another's fleas. Since we all watch, I'd venture that we do share a secret faith, against Papouli's skepticism. Mamouli's yearning tickles the soles of our feet; we can feel it in our elbows, this intimation of wings, the lift of the clavicle when she perches on a roof or in a tree, so much in a trance that she doesn't notice us standing below with our breaths held, our chins lifted toward the clouds. Annie the Elephant might see her and start flapping her ears, or Dad might stop rubbing Annie's head with vegetable oil and beat his chest with a fast fluttering motion.

Mamouli's going to take off one of these days, Papouli my friend, and I'll have the record of it right here in this notebook. Wasn't it I who predicted on paper that Papouli's father, the Great Grand-Papouli, God rest his soul in seventh heaven, would continue to perform in the circus even after the so-called doctors had pronounced him "only a vegetable"? "What's *only* about a vegetable?" I wrote at the time, though I lost that notebook when the twins' Solar Wind Machine blew it off the table, opened it up and sent it flapping out my window over a field, where it burst into flame; the field caught fire, the wind blew the fire toward the farmer's barn, the fire engines screamed in from town, frightening the dairy herd, the cows leaped in their stanchions, causing their milk to sour, and we had to pay damages. Ach! That Bimbo and Bimba! Sometimes . . . But where was I?

Here I was laughing at Mamouli right along with the others, while Papouli, who never knows when to stop — quite often he should stop just before he begins — went on piling one bad joke on another at his wife's expense, while she rubbed her hand over her brow and pretended that her great body was heaving with laughter, though we knew she was just trying to hide the tears.

Papouli told her she shouldn't slight the tightrope, after it had given so many years of faithful service, by talking about giving it up. "If you know the secret of rising, don't hog all the glory. Teach the rope. You can take a leave of absence, if you like, and go to India to consult with a genuine fakir." (He pronounced it "faker.") "When you return, you'll know how to toot the flute so seductively our tightrope will rise right out of its basket and string itself up of its own accord. You'll save poor overworked Bobby a lot of climbing."

This reference to yours truly gave me a chance to draw fire. I quickly offered an opinion I knew would divert his scorn. I said that Mamouli should indeed visit India because a place existed over there called The Vale of Kashmir, where holy men went to sit on a rock.

"And what kind of talent does this rock have, Bobby boy?"

"It juts out from a cliff over this steaming valley. If the holy men sit on it long enough they suddenly zap off into the blue and vanish."

"Do they, now? Well, let's wish them a nice trip and hope they show up in time for supper. Meanwhile, I think we'd prefer one of your more down-to-earth opinions. Something you didn't learn from your exalted YMCA guru."

He forgot that my guru was a secret between us, so I changed the subject fast. I suggested we could grab Boomie's boyfriend when he left the wagon to take a leak or something, and then we could not exactly do him in but just take him for a long ride and have him disappear. "I'm only joking," I hastened to add when I saw the exasperation on Papouli's face.

He took a deep breath, scratched his huge round stomach, and folded his arms high over his hairy chest. "Next."

The twins spoke up in properly serious tones. I can never tell when it's Bimbo talking or when it's Bimba or when the Papouli children are both talking at once. They're barely into their teens, and they still look like the kind of curly-haired cherubs you see carved in a choir loft, but they're the opposite of innocent, that's for sure. I don't doubt they'll fix the world some day through the invention of a machine that transforms consciousness. I only hope it's a quiet device. Everything they've invented so far makes so damn much noise and smells so bad. I have never been able to identify salvation with fires, wind blasts, fumes and explosions.

The invention the twins are onto now is supposed to revolutionize the carnival industry. All that's left to make is the springing device, and that can be copied from the cannon. Equilibrium is the twins' métier. They twirl at the end of the long bar during Papouli's walk on the highwire. They are the secret of his balance. They perform magical exchanges on the trapeze; they're learning how to vanish into smoke during the final triple alchemical aerial pouring exchange (I can't tell their secret here, I'm not even allowed to tell you whether I know their secret). They're the circus mechanics, experts at tuning motors, chakras and musical instruments. And now, since Polyphemus has undertaken to educate them in quantum mechanics, they have become inventors. Their dandy little machine, as they call it, is to be officially billed the Black Hole in Space, though we all have our fancy names for it, such as the Narcissus Loop or the Animus Animal. I, with my crude sense of humor, prefer to call it the Machine from Racine (concave or convex it will fit either sex and wipe itself off in between, ho ho). This as yet untested carnival ride puts couples side by side in a single chair, explodes them out of the darkness into a blinding white light, loops them to the left, sucks them back into the black hole from behind and shoots them out the front again for a loop to the right. A figure eight designed to give the riders a rush into androgyny, swinging them from male to female and back again a hundred times or so, until they emerge entirely yin-yang, intellect and intuition in precise balance. The twins' idea now was to make Boomie and her lover our first guinea pigs, in hopes they'd come out sufficient unto themselves, no longer needing each other.

"How long would the effect last?" Papouli asked, taking them seriously just to be polite.

"A year, maybe two," said Bimbo and Bimba.

"Two months at least, or at least a month," said Bimba and Bimbo. "A day, two days. Two hours, an hour. Long enough, and maybe forever," they said.

"Or not at all," said their father.

"Aw, Pop."

"Don't give me your awpopsies. Just give me some good, solid advice on how to deal with this situation. I don't doubt your machine might balance Boomie for a little while, but then she'll start to wobble. It'll all come back to her. She'll feel hot and bothered again. She'll look around for relief and see she's been jilted. Abandoned by her lover. Then watch out, folks, because she's liable to throw a boomerang right into her neck. Your machine'll be her guillotine. Look at the facts, children. When Boomie loses her lover, we lose a part of Boomie."

Papouli was referring to the time he carried Boomie's first lover out to the highway and dumped him. She boomeranged her ankle the next night. The second lover was allowed to stay, useless as he was to the rest of us. ("We could use him as the peg in a game of ring toss, that's about it," Papouli joked.) He-Power, as we called him, left of his own accord because he was bored with nothing to do but take care of the pet he kept in his pants. Boomie then chopped off her arm.

"Her mutilations may lend a certain gory publicity to her act," said Papouli, "but it absolutely can't happen again, and there's only one way to keep her satisfied."

"That's to let her have a man who's a permanent part of the circus," Mamouli said.

"That's to let her have a man who's a permanent part of the circus," said Papouli.

"But how?" asked the twins. "The seventh spot?"

"No punk kid Boomie picked up in a ditch is going to know how to fill the place my father left open."

"Now, now," said Mamouli. "Let's not pass judgment before we've met the lad. Bobby was just a punk kid when he first joined us, and look at him now."

"Yeah, look at him. Barely able to hold his own at the bottom of the heap. He's the unfunniest clown since Grant Wood's farmer."

"Thanks a lot," says I.

"Well, we're talking about the top position. It's too high. We've auditioned the very best in the world. Some of them might have left their bodies and still kept the connection. They might have gone out and come back, but you couldn't see a thing. It was boring as entertainment."

"Why wasn't Great Grand-Papouli boring?" Bimba asked. "He just lay there."

"He didn't just lie there. He listened to the harmony of the spheres. People brought their binoculars just to stare at his smile. The fact that he'd been unconscious all those years added to his attraction, of course, but it was his reputation and presence, and the beauty of that smile. Its transfiguration."

"Boomie's lover could fill one of our six spots," ventured Mamouli, "and one of us could go to the top to be transfigured."

"You never give up, do you, sweetheart. Transfiguration just happens when it happens. You can't go around on rooftops trying to figure out the technique. Besides, who's going to fill the heart spot if you ascend? An earth mother's as hard to find today as a thirty-year-old virgin showgirl."

"Chauvinist!"

17

"Exhibitionist!"

"Power hungry!"

"Glory thirsty!"

Polyphemus stood up calmly, walked over to Mamouli and Papouli and laid his huge hands on their shoulders. "Calm down now. Listen. It's going to have to be Boomie's lover this time for sure. We'll think of something, you'll see. We'll find him an act."

Our giant strode off to do some heavy thinking on his own. The rest of us stared at the sawdust for a long time. To break the gloom, I suggested that Boomie's boyfriend could learn how to roll over and play dead. "Fetch can do it. Why can't he?"

This time everybody except Papouli laughed. Maybe he thought I was making fun of the act the Great Grand-Papouli performed when he was alive, though I would never have mocked the old man. I revered him as much as anyone. I blushed.

Papouli's brow began to fold itself like an accordion. "You won't think it's so funny, Bobby, if we don't figure this one out. You're the one who cleans up after the acts. If Boomie comes back to the circus in the wrong mood, you'll be standing right next to her. It's in your face the blood will fly, and it'll be your job to stick her head in a bag."

I know he was upset, but I don't think Papouli had a right to use that tone with me. Nobody ever gets to talk back mean to him. He was a lot more respectful when his father was with us. The Great Grand-Papouli might never have said anything, but you watched your language when *he* was listening.

3

THE MYTH PERSISTS that Papouli and Son walked on high without a wire during the old days at Barnum-Ringling, before they fell. In all fairness to the Great Grand-Papouli, I can assure you the old man was against creating any such impression. He said the aerialist must always stay visibly in touch with the cord, which he regarded as his spiritual bond to Mother Earth. This belief was passed on from generations back and helps explain why our Papouli now wants to discourage the mother of his children from breaking her connection with the ground. When he broke that connection himself, he suffered much remorse on account of it. But in those days he still rebelled against the tradition. The idea of an invisible wire entranced him. Plastic was a new substance, however, and the Great Grand-Papouli distrusted it so thoroughly that he wouldn't even let me bring him a drink in a plastic cup, because he said it killed the water.

Just as our Papouli rejects the inventions of Bimbo and Bimba, so his father rejected Papouli's mania for novelty as a means of awakening consciousness. I was only a sideshow barker in those days and Polyphemus was one of the freaks, but we used to sit in on the Great Grand-Papouli's sermons out by the cages, and I can remember some of his words, even though I still don't entirely understand them.

"Culture is based on the search for novelty," and "civilization ends where culture begins," he said. He talked about perfecting the ancient styles, finding our mythic image, immersing ourselves in the development of "our chosen archetypical tradition." He's the one who convinced me that there's as much magic in pounding stakes as there is in somersaulting through space, though I have always puzzled over his insistence that "magic is tragic." He said it was my innate fear of magic that made me rush into comedy. When I showed him my clown, he said, "Robert, it's fine that your face likes to grin at the ground, but if you keep that downcast mouth every time you raise your face upward, you'll end up being the one with the worried look they make stand under the aerial acts waiting to break a great fall."

And he was right.

He was a lot harder with his son than he was with the rest of us. Part of the problem was that they liked to deal with tension in opposite ways. The father preferred a slack rope, while the son liked his rope tight. The father liked to slip, the son to spring. With the slack rope, one lets the calmness of the rope pass up into the body. With the tightrope, one passes one's own calmness into the agitated wire. The Great Grand-Papouli was a much more gentle and even feminine sort, for all his patriarchal appearance. He liked to be soothed by sweet music, fussed over and stroked by the pretty women who spun on the web. Until Mamouli came along, Papouli preferred to conquer and dominate his women.

These character differences led to a crisis over the question of whether or not to switch to a plastic rope. The son argued that a compromise between slack and tight had now been found, but the father refused even to try it. So our Papouli abandoned his father and started an act of his own above one of the side rings. That's where Mamouli first saw him and thought he was walking on air and fell in love with him. His act became so popular that inevitably the time came when the son was asked to play the center ring and the father had to move to one side. My stomach tightens when I think about the old man's humiliation. He quit. For months he sulked in his tent listening to his beloved Mozart on the Victrola, while his son performed ever more spectacular leaps and somersaults off the invisible wire. The more he tightened the wire, the higher he could spring, so he just kept tightening and tightening.

The courtship of the father by the son began. The Great Grand-Papouli sulked, he pouted. Finally he agreed to return to the act and to use the plastic rope, but only on condition that all virtuoso stunting be forsaken in favor of a return to the pure classical tradition. Our Papouli hated to give in on that, but he did. And I must say that it was their restraint, as they wafted slowly up and down, that gave the appearance of walking on air such awesome majesty.

Circus historians have said that the Great Grand-Papouli's bushy eyebrows created the illusion that he walked with eyes closed. Nonsense! When his son was up there on his shoulders for the finale, the old man did walk blind, maintaining perfect balance by singing to himself all four parts of one of his beloved string quartets.

Then came the night when the son pushed down too hard on the wire for the double-somersault spring onto his father's shoulders; the wire snapped and they fell. That is how The Great Papouli Circus came to be.

The son survived intact, thanks to a lifesaving performance by Mamouli, who miraculously appeared on the scene that night. But the Great Grand-Papouli never recovered consciousness. For five years he lay in a coma, his face entirely expressionless, while his son prepared a new circus of his own, vowing to find some way to keep his father not only in the act but at its very top as long as the Great Grand-Papouli still breathed.

Bimbo and Bimba, born from the union of Mamouli and Papouli, began to experiment with the stereophonic headphones just being tested at that time. As infants they were already precocious with electronic gadgets. They put one of the Mozart quartets on their tape recorder, slipped the headphones over the ears of their grandfather, then summoned us to see what had transpired.

As we gathered around the couch where the Great Grand-Papouli had lain seemingly senseless for so long, we saw a smile grow upon his face. The smile lit up his entire body, and though the eyes remained closed, the radiance continued to surround him until the music stopped and the smile faded and the light dimmed and the old man lay expressionless as before.

Every night after that, the smile and the radiance returned when we put the music to his ears. That smile convinced Papouli that we must become a mystical circus — a single body with each act representing one of the seven centers of subtle energy that resonates inside us, yoking us to the cosmos. All our acts would represent the union of Mother Earth with Creation, and our aim would be to attune our spectators to the celestial harmony. The Great Grand-Papouli would be at the top, as the one who transcends the gross body. Papouli had visited his sleeping father many times in dreams and believed the music we played him could connect our circus to the astral plane upon which he hovered as our guardian angel.

The old man was carried around the arena on a glittering litter during the opening parade of The Great Papouli Circus by Mamouli, Papouli, Bimbo and Bimba, and they set him down in the center of the Ring of the Moon. I, as our one-man band, made the music our audience heard. But the more wondrous music that awakened the peculiar light that people said encircled our tent was actually played secretly into the ears of the old man, who lay in a coma in his kingly robe, with his head deep in a golden pillow so that the earphones could not be seen.

Until his death, the Great Grand-Papouli kept the wildest action in the tent under control simply by lying still and breathing and listening. Who knows how many years he would have lasted if we had just played him the string quartets; but one morning the twins couldn't resist playing him a childlike, unearthly adagio for glass harmonica that Mozart had composed for an American lady shortly before he died. The tug upward was too strong.

For the first time since he fell, the Great Grand-Papouli

opened his crystal-clear eyes. All day he gazed at us. Just before we were to carry him into the tent, his mouth bent into the tightest grin we had ever seen. He sprang entirely out of his body. The mouth went slack.

We carried him into the tent.

Such was our sorrow and fear that we found ourselves sitting on the curb of the Moon Ring weeping like lost children, unable to rise and perform.

But the audience came through. When they realized that the old man was lying there lifeless on his bier, everyone in the stands stood and held hands in a great circle. Shaky and dispirited as we were, they lifted us up. We performed calmly and well.

None of us was hurt. None of us fell.

Excuse me while I close this notebook to enjoy my grief. Then I'm going into town, ostensibly to pick up the mail but also to attend a class I'm secretly taking to prepare myself for the big surprise I have in store for Mamouli.

4

I AM EAGER and ready to learn, as I sit on a gym mat inhaling the fragrance of sweaty socks, in a handball court of the town's YMCA, where I've arrived early for instruction. While I'm waiting for the others, I can enjoy writing in my notebook. An important drama is about to unfold for us, so I better start making proper introductions.

• •

My name is Robert Tertullian. They call me Bob the Grip. In the circus body I am at the bottom, at the base of the spine. My element is earth, my concern is territory. I'm in charge of setting up the tent, maintaining it, taking it down, packing it up, and moving on. I handle the ropes and the props. I clean the dung. I send out publicity, I sell the tickets. I'm the security guard, first to get up and last to go to bed. I pay fees and bribes, I order the food, I'm stage manager, collector of memorabilia and, as in these pages, the keeper of records. This makes me a very materialistic sort, and I have to work hard to compensate, by seeing to it that the grounds are always beautiful wherever we settle, that we leave our camp more lovely than we found it, that we are not greedy with the take and that what we receive is generously spent.

Most of my circus acts are not worth mentioning, since I serve primarily as an assistant who delivers and receives paraphernalia. I stand below the other acts as a kind of ground, and to break a fall if (God forbid) that should ever occur. I check the ropes, tighten the screws, supervise the concessionaires and make sure everything's cooking and popping and jingling properly behind the stands. This may seem like an impossible task, but ours is a small circus, remember, and I have plenty of help from the others and from roustabouts hired from the local population.

I even have time to perform a few funny little numbers. Sometimes I play the clown with the exploding pants, or Boomie cracks the buttons off my suspenders with her bullwhip, and my pants fall down. The point is, my buttocks are cruelly exposed. The crowd loves that, because I happen to have what you might call an exceedingly well-developed bum.

I'm not bad as a one-man band, now that the twins have built me a good sound system. The animal I'm in charge of is Fetch, a brilliant German shepherd much keener than I am in almost every regard. Fetch runs the poodle act. I only coached him a little, the way Polyphemus coached Calypso with the lady lions, though I don't put on the pretense of getting into the ring just to stand there in some fancy costume looking like a master. I don't have time for fakery. I'm too busy doing other things. Fetch hasn't needed me for a long time, and I'm glad of it. I have a theory, anyhow, that the animals are going to become masters of the earth again, with their own kind of circus. The thirty-three female poodles Fetch is in charge of know so much more than any of us about having fun that just watching them makes us nostalgic for the ancient days when we were still "at play in the fields of the Lord." I won't try to imitate the barks and growls that name them all. I'll only say that I can't imagine sleeping again in any other way than in a heap of happy poodles, now that I'm used to their warm and cuddly presences.

My appearance? I'm short and thick and strong as a bull, and when the local kids I hire get mad because I'm so demanding, they call me Dirty Bob. I guess I don't wash much, but what's the point when I'm back in the dirt right away, anyhow? The kids end up loving me because I give them prizes, and the ones who hang around never have much trouble sneaking past me. I even come out of the ticket booth sometimes to show the timid ones where there's a hole in the tent.

Boomie and I spent several years of our childhood together. She broke my heart. I won't dwell on it. She's broken so many others. She doesn't even make me jealous (much), the way she does another certain one of us. Papouli says that Boomie could never really fall in love, because her energy flows upward and the energy of love must flow down, must fall "into the pool of incarnation." As for Mamouli, I don't know whether it would be more correct to say that I love her or that I'm in love with her. Certainly I would never dream of trying to win her away from Papouli, but sometimes I do yearn terribly to give her the kind of tenderness he has failed to show in recent years, though I know he loves her immensely.

My current way of expressing my feelings for Mamouli is to prepare a big surprise for her. That's why I'm here bright and early at the Y. Bob the Grip is going to show Mamouli how to rise. Granted, the method I'm learning takes you up fast and brings you down hard, and Mamouli wants to rise with the slow elegance of a preening saint — she wants to hover and show off while she's up there. But at least I'll prove to her that you can get off the ground, and that should raise her spirits, if nothing else.

I've been sneaking over here to take a crash course in the sudden school of levitation from a weightlifting instructor who's also an accredited meditator. He's teachng us — don't laugh — how to bump along on our butts. Papouli's the only one in the family who knows what I'm up to, and I'm not going to tell him any more until I'm ready to give a demonstration to Mamouli.

Papouli says all I'm doing is learning a method of involuntary thigh flapping. "I hope you do show her," he says, "so she'll see how ludicrous the whole affair really is."

If you want my opinion, I'd say Papouli is just a little afraid old bottom-of-the-totem-pole Bobby is going to find out something he doesn't know and pass it on to Mamouli, and then she'll rise higher than him and they'll start calling it The Great Mamouli Circus.

How do you like them apples?

The guy here at the Y is teaching me a form of sitting

levitation that avoids a crucial error made by all the other gurus. The others all want you to start by awakening the kundalini serpent said to be curled up asleep at the base of the spine. That's wrong. She's wide awake.

The kundalini has been a virtual insomniac for the last two thousand years, at least in the Western world. You have to lull her to sleep, don't you see? Get her to curl up in a nice tight coil down there where the sacrum (the holy bone) joins the ilium. Then drone your mantra over and over again until she becomes so bored with it she dozes off. Send the hum of the mantra down deeper and deeper until you can actually hear the kundalini snoring. Then shout out a sudden warning. Fire! Murder! Scream as if you were having a primal Tarzanic orgasm. The kundalini awakes with a start, terrified. She tries to spring up out of your body so fast that the hole at the top of your head doesn't have time to open. The energy backfires and you blast off. It's as simple as that.

Sorry I can't tell you the mantra. You have to pay a high price for one. Not in the crass commercial sense, but to prove you're serious. And you need a private in- terview with the instructor. He has to feel your kunda- lini — that's the embarrassing part of the course. But worth it. Downstairs in his office, amongst the trophies, swimming charts and ping-pong paddles, you have to bend over his desk and let him explore your sacroiliac so he can decide exactly what kind of serpent you have stir- ring about down there and what kind of sound will put her to sleep. He himself tries out various bass and treble moans with his vibrating fingers, until he finds the one that seems to work.

Let me not make false claims, however. Thus far I only

know how to pop up like a piece of toast. I don't skid along the gym mat yet, like the more advanced students. They really know how to bump around. You can smell their shorts scorching.

At the end of each session we are a jolly, self-congratulatory bunch, sore in the behind but feeling much more confident up front as we return to our various endeavors. We bow before we leave the handball court, in deference to our teacher's guru, who can be seen (fast photography, Papouli says) in a picture on the gallery wall, seated a good foot off the floor and looking heavenward toward his own guru, who is said to have shot up into the sky and never come down. Went into orbit, Papouli says; which is why I'm keeping this to myself from now on, until I'm ready. Then, Mamouli, watch your old Bobby show you how it's done. If I can sit on air for even an instant, surely you'll figure out how to walk on the stuff.

Ah! Here come the others. I can hear their laughter in the hall.

5

YOU WOULDN'T BELIEVE the pressure junk-food hucksters put on us concessionaires. They rush to the rescue with their trash the moment they sense disaster. I'm being courted by the hot dog and hamburger people. The mailbox is full of ads for sugar that's spun and whipped and hidden in the condiments. Am I imagining things, or has this last piece of mail been scented with chocolate? Damn! And me with my predilection for pressure, my joy in junk. It's their fault I went over to the drugstore after levitation and pigged out.

The temptations they wave under my nose make me so mad. Why can't they get it through their thick skulls we're a mystical circus opposed to the exploitation of violence? I don't care how bad the gate is, we simply cannot allow sugar or salt in our tent. We dispense unsalted popcorn, apples, bran muffins, carob candy and honeyed lemonade, that's all — and these are only to be consumed under the stands.

Sometimes our customers tear at their hair trying to find a refreshment booth with the junk they're used to. They kick the dirt and scream for their money back. Without the usual concessions, we have to be very, very good out there just to hold our audience; so good that when people watch us and their mouths drop open they lose the impulse to stuff something into them. Our aim is not to awaken a need to smother or choke oneself but to let in plenty of good fresh air, which stirs the breast to mirth and allows the deep gasp of amazement.

The trouble is that nobody's gasping these days. Without Boomie, they're bored. All the acts we thought were death-defying turn out to be deadly dull, compared to the way they were when everybody in the stands was sexually aroused. Now there are gangs roaming about under the stands, searching for some kind of satisfaction. If you think I haven't been tempted to call in the soft-drink trucks, take a look at this letter. It doesn't even apply to our circus, and they sent it anyway. Some of these distributors know I'm a clown. That must be it. They're trying to make me laugh. There's a handwritten note at the top that says, "Howdy, Bob. We hear you're not doing too good."

> Dear Management: [that's me]
> This is to remind you that your concession stands much more than our big studios are the true producers of the entertainments we provide. We can only supply the demand your refreshments induce. If you do not first put the stuff of shock into your customers, how can you expect us to shock them?
> *The munchie is the message.*
> Get those soft drinks into the blood stream. We'll do the

rest. Remember: sugar is shock. Sugar is rage. The shock is not on stage or screen. It's projected out there by the body.

As for tension, we remind you once again that we cannot produce it. We can only prolong the tension salt induces. It's up to you to raise that blood pressure.

So salt your popcorn, hawk those salty dogs, and we'll promise you a thriller every time. Sell the big cup, push the big box, watch our entertainments explode on stage and screen!

Christ! We don't want to send our audience home packed tight with rage. We want to release the pressure. We're having trouble enough keeping everybody calm as it is. "Boomie! Boomie!" they chant, until Pegasus trips and Annie almost steps on my head and the lions forget they're only supposed to *act* vicious. The Papoulis are the only ones who can keep them quiet. How can you love an audience you're beginning to hate? Hooligans! Rowdies!

But here I am working up my own rage, blaming our spectators for the situation we ourselves have created. Bob the Grip, get a grip on yourself. You should be ashamed. It's that giant triple dip hot fudge sundae you had in town, with the foot-long hot dog and the colossal Coke. If Papouli knew you broke the salt and sugar agreements every time you went into town, he'd be furious. The tension better be out of your system by performance time tomorrow night.

Tension is the one great sin of our circus. It contradicts our essential purpose. Tension is the opposite of attention, you see. Our country is full of performers and audiences building up tension, making each other sick. Performers popping pills, audiences stuffing themselves and screaming. Directors screaming too. Frantic actors. Frayed viewers. Musicians on stage throwing glorified tantrums or belting out their anguish at everybody within range of their sound systems. It's hideous to see these suicidal heroes taking over the entertainment world. We want no part of it. The best performers are always those who have mastered the art of effortless a-tension. If Papouli's body were tense when he stepped on the wire, the wire would shudder so violently he could never gain his balance. The wire attends to his wishes when he transfers his calmness into it. Later in the act he makes the wire tense, but that's because he knows the audience has learned to still the wire with a calmness of its own. We try to share the circus magic, taking the spectator into that graceful dimension where everything occurs with the greatest of ease.

Watch any of our performers and you'll see that we work in a relaxed way. That's why people sit up so straight. Energy flows easily up and down the spine. There's no need either to slouch in one's chair or to leap up and cheer. At the peak of each performance we like to see our spectators rise smoothly and easily, with wonder in their eyes. We want their applause to sound like a wave rolling across a marvelous beach, before it withdraws with a great inhalation and everyone settles back again in rapt amazement. Perhaps the best circuses — those concerned with equilibrium — are going out of style because audiences have been trained to confuse attention with strain. Strain leads to pain, pain leads to hunger for relief, and this hunger leads to diseases caused by consumption. There can be no serenity in an audience of consumers consumed by craving.

I think all of us here at the circus are trying too hard these days. We're such phonies outside the tent, forgetting what we know; working up all sorts of tension because we're trying to grasp the situation instead of just letting it work itself out. I'll bet Boomie and her lover aren't uptight about it. They're probably lying on her bed while the rest of us worry. Boomie's probably sound asleep in that young man's arms while he strokes her hair and gazes contentedly at the ceiling, unaware of all the anxiety and hope his presence has provoked. The lucky bastard.

6

PAPOULI OFTEN TALKS of setting forth in his old age for the island in the river, surrounded by cliffs, where tightrope walkers go to spend their last days. Nobody will be able to reach him there unless they, too, can walk the cable over the windy abyss. He'll be in his cave alone, with nobody to talk to and nothing to do but gaze at the birds and watch the roiling waters. Then he'll want to remember everything that happened, and he'll open the package I send on the little trolley attached to the cable, and he'll read of our adventures.

My notebooks should bring more than a few smiles of recognition to Papouli's big, round, rough old mustached face. If I'm a bit hard on him at times, I know he'll forgive me (won't you, Papouli?). So far, most of our adventures have started out in a rather tragic way, but they are always redeemed by comedy. I am a firm believer that comedy rules the world. God laughs and plays and has his little jokes, and who are we to catch on to them all? Certainly humans and beasts have one thing in common: We like to get ourselves into trouble just so we can find our way out again. Trouble puts us to the test.

Papouli always likes to make it seem as if we were once more on the precarious edge — but he only plays with suspense, don't you see? That's what's so much fun. It's part of his act, just as mine is to chew at a problem the way a puppy chews at a tasty bone.

Papouli pretends we're in trouble with the Boomie situation, and I pretend to believe it. In fact I do believe it, just as I continue to believe every night that he and his whole family are going to fall from on high when the wire goes crazy, though I know perfectly well in another part of me that as long as there's an audience there can be no fall.

You see, the Papoulis could not be the spectacular act they are if they did not lose control at a certain point. Without the loss of control there would be no gasp from the crowd, and without the gasp the breath would not be held. If the breath were not held, the wire would not be stilled; and if the wire were not stilled the Papouli family would indeed fall. There being no net, it would be byebye Bimbo, Bimba, Mamouli and Papouli.

The creation of precarious situations is the reason for the success of this circus. I may not be as smart as the others, but I certainly understand that. I also understand that a performer cannot be an attraction while suffering from distraction, unless that distraction is recognized as a greater attraction, treated as such and somehow brought into the arena. An outside distraction has to become an inside attraction, get me? Or there's big trouble. You can't be in charge of security without a preventive sense of mishap. You have to study the body of each performer for the signs. I'll keep a close eye on Boomie when she rejoins us. If she tenses up again, she's had it. I'd have to be very alert to save her if she threw a boomerang off course. There's probably not much I could do, should she lose another lover. Self-mutilation would be inevitable.

What else can you expect from a woman who likes to throw knives at herself for a living? If the lover leaves, we lose Boomie, or at least a big enough part of her so that I don't think she'd be performing any more. And how could we endure the sorrow? For we have become so much one body that any injury to her would be an equal injury to us all. Am I being sentimental? I think not.

What we do for our spectators is tune their bodies. That is why there are six of us, like six strings on a guitar. Once we had the much more special resonance of a seven-string guitar. The music we made then, with the Great Grand-Papouli as our star, made people sit up as straight as the tent's two main masts, between which Papouli walks on the wire. We had them sailing off into bliss; they were literally out of their heads as they left the tent, looking neither right nor left, erect and directed toward the highest good, adults and children alike, walking home in happy trances.

By tuning all seven centers of the subtle body (known in yoga as the chakras), we brought the audience into such communion with us that it seemed as if our acts sprang from their imaginations and were sustained by the perfect beauty of their vision. But that was when we had entered a state of grace. Who can say how one slips into grace and out again? Our reputation from those days still lingers with us. Until this latest problem with Boomie, people expected so much they wouldn't allow themselves to think they hadn't experienced this communion. But we have known for some time that, good as we still are, our acts are no longer performed with what Papouli calls "the maximum of aplomb."

Boomie is aware of her responsibility in this, and I know she doesn't want her passion to destroy us this time, any more than she did the times before. Quite the opposite. Her body may have chosen lovers that her mind should have regretted, but she really does want to provide emotional stability not only for herself but for the rest of us. She knows she needs a lover who can fill the seventh spot, unless one of us can find a way to the top, in which case her man can try for the role left vacant lower down. We're all working at it, except Polyphemus. Everybody knows you can't transcend wisdom unless you're willing to play the complete fool. Our giant had enough of that during his days as a freak.

It's someone who performs at the inspired level of a compleat idiot we need now — somebody willing to perform in a way that seems entirely senseless, devoid of all good judgment. A serious old sage like Papouli's father only got out of his body because he was knocked out of it, knocked permanently senseless. Our new man will have to rise above himself, yet recover his senses after every performance. He'll need the resilience of one of those balloon men with sand in the bottom who pop right up though you knock them down a thousand times. Boomie's second lover was like that, but in a exclusively genital way.

Her first lover was an extremely charming fellow whom I personally liked a lot. I think he made Papouli jealous. Anyhow, our chief tricked him into hoisting himself on his own petard. When this fellow saw there was no act for him in the tent, he figured out a way to entertain people as they entered the circus grounds. He billed himself as the Fastest Comb in the West. Wearing a cowboy outfit with long black combs sticking out of both pockets, he would challenge men and boys to fast-comb contests. He never lost. Plugged them in the heart every time, before they could even get a grip on their comb. But they loved him and had it out with one another for the privilege of challenging him. Combs were flying all over the field. Then one night when the Fastest Comb in the West was sitting across the poker table from Papouli, he began to do a little innocent boasting about some of the tricks Boomie had by way of making love. Papouli turned red, slammed his fist down on the table so hard the chips leaped to the floor, and muttered that if he ever heard such talk again he'd get his gun and shoot him down on the spot.

A few weeks later, the Comb (as we called him) was boasting again over by the corral when Papouli walked up unseen, overheard, and strode off toward his wagon. He reappeared shortly with fire in his eyes.

"I told you what I'd do if you ever dared talk that way about Boomie," Papouli said, snarling.

"Aw, come on," said the Comb, backing away as he saw Papouli slip a hand into the vest pocket under his ringmaster's coat.

"Take that, you son of a bitch!" Papouli pulled out his weapon and fired.

The Fastest Comb in the West clutched at his heart and toppled flat on his face in the mud. Papouli picked him up, whistled for Pegasus, slung him over the saddle, mounted the horse's rump and took Boomie's lover all the way to the highway, where he dumped him against a fence. When the poor fellow revived from his faint and realized he'd been shot by a comb, he must have been too ashamed to return.

• •

Boomie's second lover was completely insane, just as Papouli's book said a seventh chakra performer must be. But this dude's split personality made us just too uncomfortable. Papouli nicknamed him He-Power Big because he was only happy when seated at his organ. I don't doubt that the organ in question (on display is more accurate) gave Boomie a lot of pleasure. Though He-Power himself seemed a dull sort, who but Boomie can say how bright a creature the organ was when it went into action. We only saw it when it was lazing around on He-Power's lap, being petted and pampered.

He-Power couldn't give Boomie the love she needed. He couldn't even love himself. All his love was reserved for the organ that, before being brought to our circus, had performed in numerous films and on stage, first in Tijuana, later in Los Angeles and San Francisco, and finally, for a star-studded year, at the Follies Bérgères, which He-Power forsook to cross the ocean in search of the woman the great French lovers were always raving about.

When He-Power and his pet weren't entertaining Boomie, one could most often find them in the costume truck. He-Power would be seated on a bench in front of his locker with the fat, sleepy beast slumped over the palm of his hand, belly down, snoozing. On the upper shelf of the locker were various oils, ointments and powders. On the inside of the door were taped stills of the organ at work in the movies. He-Power would sit gazing down on his beloved pet sprawled out in a dream that occasionally made it twitch. Then he would stroke it and murmur endearments. I used to watch a woman at Barnum-Ringling treat her chubby little trained weasel that way.

He-Power conversed with the rest of us in a pleasant enough way, though he used to shush us rudely if we talked too loud. Meanwhile, he'd be stroking the organ on the back or tickling it behind the neck. Sometimes he'd rub it down with oil or give it a smooth coat of scented talc. There was no question of putting this creature in the circus, Papouli said. Anyone could see it was too swell-headed. It would never be willing to start from the bottom and work its way up.

He-Power and his pet hung around until they grew to resent Boomie. They figured she had ruined them for other women. Finally, Polyphemus, whose modesty they offended, told a story about a perfect beauty named Circe living on one of the Greek islands. Not even the giants had been able to satisfy her. He-Power's organ raised up and gleamed when it heard this. Despite its owner's protestations, it insisted on being packed up and taken on a new search. Who knows what it might have done otherwise — bit him or strangled him, I suppose.

Ever since, Polyphemus has been feeling culpable for the loss of Boomie's arm. But I think her second lover would have left anyhow. He resented us and we resented him. Besides, he was a pure and simple fool. What we need is someone who only fakes a fool.

7

To fake a fool, you have to know how to fake a fall — how to fall without really falling. That's one of the hardest acts there is, because it can only *seem* tragic. In a circus each performer has to know how to bounce back on his feet, how to bring off a comic outcome.

Boomie has ventured as near to the edge as we care to imagine. She has made her wounds attractive. Who else can do that — except a Christ, of course — and how can this fellow we last glimpsed lying in a ditch represent the highest of all the energy centers, the one yogis and shamans and medicine women from all the sacred tribes only dare hint at?

None of us doubts that a mysterious opening exists at the top of the head, through which the Great Spirit, which lives in us all, leaves the unconscious body and returns. The Great Grand-Papouli passed through the opening by accident. But how to do it by design?

One hint comes from certain American Indian and Tibetan tribes who keep a clown dancing over the hole in the dome of the sacred lodge while the elders inside make the music that keeps the moon and sun and stars in their orbits. I am not that kind of clown and I never could be. My act is necessarily vulgar. In mystical terms, I represent the divine in the ordinary. We need someone more in the tradition of the extraordinary: the holy fool. Plenty of clowns of this type have auditioned for us over the last few years.

Bob Bly, the Leaping Poet, certainly lifted us all up when he wore his masks and spun and sang, but people expect us to perform in silence and they don't know how to watch words take flight. Tom Trip the Space Cadet brought his own sound system, and the sound effects he produced by smashing his guitar did blast us beyond the sound barrier into a state of deafness where all we could hear for hours was a distant ringing in the ears. He assured us that he had traveled that distance and rung those bells from wherever he had gone, but all we saw was a very spectacular tantrum. If only we could have been half as amazed at what he did as he was amazed at himself. His mistake was in blowing *his* mind instead of blowing ours.

For the art of being flung about, I preferred the skinny woman in the calico dress. She claimed it was God who seized her and shook her and caused her to shriek. We believed it. Papouli insisted, however, that making love to God in public belongs in the revival tent and not in the circus tent, where, out of context, it seems too obscene.

A more subtle audition was performed by a kindly, bespectacled gentleman whose only costume was a big red artificial nose. He managed to fool us for a while simply by sitting in the Sun Ring with eyes closed, while he carried on out-of-the-body flirtations by whispering into the ears of a great number of women in our audience. The tizzy he raised was something to hear, and we were quite disappointed to discover he was nothing but a dirty old ventriloquist trying to make dummies of us all.

Some of the laughing swamis, with impressive luster in their eyes, dropped in to see us. But when they found there was no way to get rich in our kind of circus they giggled merrily, wished us the best and, without even bothering to show us their stuff, got back into their long black cars and signaled their chauffeurs to drive on.

The only performer who really might have worked out was a powerful Slavic farmer who had won the hammerthrow in the Olympics and then had had his spiritual eye opened when he collapsed of sunstroke while trying to win a hero's medal at harvesting. Dazed, he wandered away toward Turkestan, where he was taken in by the whirling dervishes, who initiated him and sent him back home with instructions to apply his new religion to the common labor he had abandoned. He returned to the fields, where he undertook to mow hay with a heavy sickle tied to a rope. Whirling round and round, he mowed down great golden circles of grain, and would have continued in this occupation had he not been tempted by a report of Boomie from one of the pilgrims who had crossed half the world to see her and stopped to rest at the edge of the field, on his way back to Leningrad. The Golden Sickle showed us how he would glean the energy of the people, generating a cosmic wind in our tent that would lift the action right off

46

the ground. He would stand in the center of the Ring of the Sun with his long golden blade and whirl continuously during our entire show. The catch was that he wanted Boomie. She was never one for the muscular type. Also, we felt that we shouldn't take him away from the valuable work he was performing out-of-doors amidst a vast, adoring proletariat. So that his feelings wouldn't be too hurt, Papouli told him that the West tends to corrupt too many genuine stars of the East and that we couldn't in good conscience be a part of it. That was no lie. It's a pity.

There's nothing to do but hope Boomie's lover can come through where others have failed. We can't allow him to leave us. Of course, we won't put him in a cage. I've already explained our view of cages. He'll have to choose to be with us. He'll have to accept the act Papouli assigns him, if an act can be conceived. He'll have to take a great liking to us right away. We'll have to seduce him not only into allegiance but into love.

That won't be so hard. Or will it?

I look out my window and see the light still on in the Papouli wagon. Papouli and Dad have been seated on their porch all this time ruminating. I never go to bed before they do. Since they may well spend the whole night trying to get a handle on our problem, I'll just introduce some of our cast while I wait.

First, I'm going to let the dogs out for a run. Fetch and the poodles have never been able to sleep until I bed myself down with them. They'll just be lying there restlessly counting sheep, and this isn't even sheep country. Nobody's going to shoot them out there. To hell with keeping them penned up.

8

INTRODUCING JOHN M. PAPOULI: Ringmaster, owner and star performer of The Great Papouli Circus. Author of *The Velvet Tightrope*, a book on mystical mechanics, which the twins claim was written mostly by them (sorry, Papouli, but that's what they say), and *The Compleat Idiot's Guide to Walking on Air*, a cautionary manual published to discourage what Papouli considers the dangerous ambitions of a large number of people, including his circus family, who suffer from what he calls "angelism."

According to Papouli, the mystics have it all wrong. The great feat is not to leave your body but to get into it properly:

> The mystical body, like any other, is still in need of a good mechanic. Heaven is a land of spiritual failures whose confusion keeps them from getting down to the

business of creating solid forms and inhabiting them. Transcendence is chaos whirling about in unfulfilled yearning for the triumph of cosmic immanence, and only an idiot who lives outside of thought, in the realm of pure images, could hope to walk on air — this by entering into a self-conceived image of himself as someone magically endowed, then sticking to the image the way light does to chemically treated paper, until the mental chemistry finally fades and one vanishes forever into the spooky, unearthly insane asylum of the numinous.

Papouli had to publish the books himself. They have an arrogant tone that puts publishers off. Mamouli says the first book encourages false hope in salvation through machinery, and the second only tells the reader not to do what she has already done without ever having acted the least bit idiotic, let alone having vanished.

I'll stay out of the argument except to say that I've noticed how often people in power deceive themselves into thinking they're the brains of the outfit. They're always surprised and even hurt when, having fired the quiet one who really does the thinking for them, the business begins to collapse. Let's hope Papouli doesn't altogether forget that most of the brilliant ideas he takes credit for come from Polyphemus. And Polyphemus closed both books after reading page one.

Power, not thought, is Papouli's forte. One look at his gut and you'd know that. Power is located in the stomach. Its element is fire. Papouli is not quite as big as a sumi wrestler, but he's built on that order, and though there's much chicanery in the wrestling match he has with Dad, he still has to be mighty strong to throw that big gorilla around.

Papouli's curly blond hair and walrus mustache and his sideburns well below the ears make him look like a wrestler by the name of Gorgeous George, who used to appear on television. Papouli can put on the same effeminate mince when he walks up to Annie the Elephant, bends under her and lifts her off the ground on his back.

Another image that comes to mind is that of the fat man in the pink tights you see in so many paintings of Picasso's *saltimbanques* series. Picasso is Papouli's artistic saint. (Chagall is Mamouli's.) If you saw us all together standing around our chief in a field with the animals nearby, you'd take us for something out of the rose period.

Papouli conceived of the circus, chose and trained its cast and imposed its discipline, though he is by far more demanding of himself than he is of others. The fat on his body is misleading. He's solid as a rock. He does his Tai Chi every morning; and nobody's supposed to know this because it embarrasses him, but we found out the reason he grows his own vegetables in the greenhouse on the flatbed truck that travels with us is that he will only eat greens and roots fertilized by his own excrement. Like many circus people, he drinks his own urine, and it is rumored that he practices retention of semen in sex. I know he finds me vulgar for talking about this, but for some reason these austerities fascinate me. Since I only play the clown, I practice no austerities whatsoever.

Papouli never goes to bed without making the rounds of the camp, checking on everyone to make sure they're in high spirits, tucking them in and kissing them goodnight. He may be stern during the day, but at night he leaves a ripple of laughter in his wake. In the tent, too, the laughter at the finale belongs to him. The show closes with Mamouli, the twins and Papouli in their pink and blue tights standing on the platform at the east end of the highwire, forty-seven feet above the Ring of the Sun. Papouli takes hold of the balancing pole and grips it against his chest, and the twins handwalk it in perfect balance until they have reached either extreme, where they lower themselves, clamp their mouths over a bit and, with hands behind their backs, begin to twirl. Mamouli climbs up on Papouli's shoulders. Papouli, lithe in his hugeness, with the equally huge Mamouli gripping his neck with her thighs, almost leaps out onto the wire, and slides down it, zip, with his whole family, right to the center, where he comes to an abrupt stop.

I, who stand below, throw up the seven golden balls, which Mamouli catches one by one, juggling them in a higher and higher arc while Bimbo and Bimba continue to whirl and swirl, hanging by their teeth, their arms out now, their bodies like propellers at the end of the pole.

As I said before, the act would not be all that spectacular if Papouli did not lose control of the wire. Perhaps you expect me to say that he merely *appears* to lose control. Not at all. The control is lost, my friends. There is only one way to get that wire back to steady once Papouli's legs begin to wobble and the whole construction goes berserk. The wire sways so far from side to side that at one point the performers are leaning almost parallel to the ground. We are within an inch of seeing the wire do a complete arc. Then it begins to wiggle and crack as well. Papouli drops into a deep, shaky-legged crouch.

Mamouli lurches to the right for a ball thrown out of

reach. She misses. Down below, I catch it and then catch the others in my shirt, while Papouli lurches to the left in a desperate bid to regain the center. And now the Papoulis are a spastic mess. The twins whip about like fish on hooks. I, who earlier asked the crowd for absolute silence, look about and see that everyone has frozen, knuckles in mouth, terror in eyes. That is when Papouli rises up too suddenly. Mamouli throws out flailing arms. The crowd gasps.

Breath is held. Breath: that is the secret.

Everybody in the tent completely concentrates on restoring the balance inside themselves. They sit upright, they send forth their own signals to balance, inward to the spine and outward to where Papouli, crouched again, rushes up the wire to catch up with the falling Mamouli. He somehow gets under her, straightens her, slides back down, finds his legs. The crowd lets out a slow sigh, causing the walls of the tent to balloon outward. Peace is restored. The wire grows still.

An enormous calm fills the tent.

I throw the golden balls back up to Mamouli. The twins whirl again, so fast you can only see whirs of pink and blue.

There is a hole at the top center of the tent through which the balls vanish into the mouth of the moon. With perfect ease, Papouli carries his family up the wire to the west platform. As the applause breaks out, the Papoulis are suddenly, with a jump backward, on the wire again. Papouli slides, zip, down and up to the opposite platform, where the act began.

Waves of laughter lift the crowd to its feet. With vast relief, tears in their eyes, they join hands, raise their arms and celebrate our common triumph. Those of us on the ground assemble in the Ring of the Sun, gesturing up to the Papoulis, source of our power. We bow.

Everyone goes home satisfied, healed.

9 ❦

OUR ORIGINS are more with medicine shows than with traditional circuses, and Mamouli is the one who keeps us healthy. She is our herbalist, cook, acupuncturist, masseuse and the bosom we like to lay our heads on. Her center of energy is the heart. Her aspect, compassionate. The twins are the only ones who were literally suckled at her breasts, but her bosom nourishes us all. She doesn't like to hear us talk about our problems (though she loves to talk about hers), but a delight that might be hard for some of you to understand, if you never had a big mama in your camp, awaits you when, feeling down in the mouth, you wander over to the Papouli wagon. If Papouli isn't there, Mamouli's liable to by lying on the bed taking her afternoon nap. Before you can tell her what's wrong, she says "Shhh!" and pats the blanket beside her, and you lie down and she pulls her blouse up, uncovering her enormous swell of soft, warm, milk-smelling breasts, and she holds your head against them saying "There, there now," and you bury your face in the warmth of her flesh, and sometimes she even lets you pop a big, plump nipple in your mouth and she says "Now, now, now." And when you leave a half-hour later you're a changed man or woman, and there's a puckered-up cupid smile on your lips. Ah, God, I love Mamouli so much. I wish with all my heart and soul, I pray every night before I go to bed, that she'll realize her dream.

When Mamouli was five years old, she was standing in the back yard of her house. It was the first really warm, sunny day of spring, and the snow was freshly melted on the lawn. She was watching a robin pull up a worm, when the robin became startled by a garbage truck in the alley and flew to the limb of the apple tree. She had an impulse to fly up with it. She crouched down with arms at her sides and fists clenched tight. Then she kind of lifted off, holding her breath and kicking her legs as if she were treading water. The next thing she knew, she was in the tree. Since that day, she has never stopped trying to walk on air.

But Mamouli lifting off? You can understand the humor of it. She weighs at least three hundred pounds. It would be like the dancing hippos in *Fantasia*. She isn't what you'd call ethereal, though she does have remarkably slim ankles and she's light on her feet. Her flesh, which smells so sweetly of warm milk, is firm and creamy smooth. She's beautiful, too, with her lustrous black curly hair and her big cow eyes. And, heavy though she may be, what Mamouli does is lighten your load. I say that with a certain apprehension. At regular intervals she performs a housecleaning that nearly kills a pack rat like me every time. Everything into the fire. One big conflagration and we journey on, clean, down again to our essential props and costumes. Mamouli has little patience with people who cling. Drop your load or you'll never fly, she says. You should see the way she flies when she's shot from the cannon. Though I know she hates the housewife marionette act Papouli puts her through, she jerks and flops and jumps about on the back of Pegasus with an amazingly comic lightness of foot.

As for juggling, it's awesome the way she sends those golden balls flying out through the hole at the top of the tent. I think she resents being carried on Papouli's shoulders for the grand finale all these years, though, getting no credit for her part in keeping the wire tuned with her humming — even being the one who appears to blow the act. The only reason she keeps going up there with him is that she hopes someday he'll step back and say, "Okay, go ahead, sweetheart, drop the wire, do it on the air."

Mamouli enjoys a special communion with the leviathans of earth and water. When we performed in Africa, hippos clambered out of the river to come have a look at her. She has sung to whales under the sea and is a proponent of the belief that the language of whales is pure musical improvisation on cosmic themes and variations. She's convinced that she herself is a cosmic whale who somehow got beached and transformed into the body of a human. She claims that Boomie's dolphins told her flying saucers aren't space vehicles at all. They're living creatures, akin to the mammal, which dart from star to star the way fish dart from rock to rock. They manufacture their food from the suns and create photosynthesis from the oxygen stored in the cells of their epidermises. The sky, Jack and Jill told her, is just another element that's easy to move in, once you get the magnetism.

Annie the Elephant shares Mamouli's beliefs. She and Mamouli are boon companions. A family joke is that they're lovers. Papouli pretends to be jealous. I guess I started the rumor myself. Shame on me! But don't you think it's funny to imagine? Never mind. Annie and Mamouli do spend a lot of time tucked up against each other. They take frequent morning hikes to the nearest railroad track, where Mamouli is teaching Annie how to walk the rail. That's how many of us accomplish our first childhood meditations, isn't it? Walking the rail is the most natural method of centering.

Mamouli hopes to make Annie the first elephant ever to walk the highwire. She wants to repay Annie for her faith. I shall have to tell you some other time about the night Mamouli crawled on her belly. When that horribly embarrassing performance was over and Mamouli was still writhing about on the stage, arms spread as if in flight, a huge grin of triumph on her pathetic face, Annie ran to her and lifted her up in her trunk and carried her on a victorious circuit of the arena, then trundled out of the tent and lay Mamouli down in the straw of the elephant pavilion, where she wrapped her trunk around the confused woman's belly, pulled her up tight and . . . what? Whispered her a lullaby?

Good old Annie. Good old Mamouli. I've gone on too long about them, and here it's almost dawn. I was going to tell about Mamouli's pity for the earth, but a few paragraphs pasted in from *The Compleat Idiot's Guide* will do quite well. Papouli gave me twenty complimentary copies, for my "edification." They were worth reading and would have sold if Papouli's many years on the highwire had not given him the bad habit of trying to stay balanced on a sentence as long as he possibly could without falling off onto a period:

I share the view of my splendid wife, the Great Mamouli, that Earth has had enough of us, she's dying and wants to be left alone, she wants us to get off, fly away, be weaned of our remorseless suckling on her poor dried up bosom; and I also agree that Earth intuited her extinction long ago and brought forth humankind in order to send her spirit to another star, settle elsewhere, lay her old soul to rest and begin again.

In other words our instinctual, human, earth-bound purpose is to serve as an organ of flight into the heavens as the only surviving expression of the particular elements that make up life as we know it, for we are the blithe spirit launched by the romantic poets who heard the ascending song of the nightingale, beheld the diminished glory of nature and, loving nature, longed to be released from her into the vast mystery from whence she had once descended; or, as the divine Wordsworth puts it, "I know where'er I go, that there hath passed away a glory from the earth . . . The Soul that rises with us, our life's Star, hath had elsewhere its setting, and cometh from afar . . ."

The Great Mamouli longs to fly in spirit to another land (don't we all, except certain inveterate groundskeepers, drillers, spelunkers and diggers?), there to plant the seed of the maternal soul, and she doesn't want to take her body with her, that's the trouble (because when you scorn the flesh you scorn the love of God that wants to incarnate itself in every nook and cranny of this universe) and, as she sees it, the struggle to get off this planet before it breathes its last is becoming radically divided between those like me who are in error because they want to cling to the substantial body and refuse to transcend it — they want to have their earth and leave it too, she says — and the spiritual forces who want to make their ascent out of the body, somehow traveling in a more subtle vehicle.

What my esteemed wife doesn't realize is that a space-craft, with its umbilical electronic connections and womb-like cabin, is the necessary fruit of which we are the seed. In the Great Mamouli's world, there are heavy, lugubrious people of my ilk tucked into weighty metal vehicles, carrying clichéd prayers in their zippered space suits, trying to fling themselves and their dirty business, briefcases and all, off the earth; and their rivals (the enlightened ones of her cosmology) who are learning, albeit even more clumsily at this stage than the astronauts, to leave the body altogether and to travel entirely free of the material element.

"Tibetan chants are the best engines," she says. The choice of vehicles can mean either celestial disaster or celestial triumph (I agree) because we are not like those creatures our dolphins are descended from who are born, live and die in the sky, subsisting on light alone and staying on the rocks only long enough to nest. We have to take off, find another rock, land softly and stay there. But my wife thinks we can just step off the ground, our flesh transformed into something insubstantial, and she's wrong just as all the saints have been wrong with their angelistic obsessions.

59

Earth first tried to transcend herself with the bird; next she tried the human imagination with its capacity for flight through inner space; and now the trick is for us to help people extend their imaginations correctly into outer space, and we have to get it right this time. That's why we at The Great Papouli Circus . . .

So, you see, Papouli feels that Mamouli is riding for a fall, and it's a great source of dispute between them. Dishes are thrown. Tables are broken. The battle always starts over the education of the twins. Papouli tries to push them toward a nice, practical, mechanical view of the world. He enrolls them in correspondence courses sponsored by polytechnic colleges. When Mamouli tries to entice them into turning their considerable talents toward pure mysticism, he goes into a rage. Their job is to keep the machinery working, he shouts. Applied mysticism, alas for Mamouli, is bound to win the day, because that's where the work is, that's what brings in the money. The best the twins can do is to seek a compromise by creating machines that help us escape the machine. They — what's that?

Gunshots? Naw, just firecrackers outside in the Boomie camp. Unless — you don't suppose they're shooting at the dogs? Better go check.

10

EVERYTHING'S FINE. Just my paranoia. Fetch and the poodles are right here around my chair now, panting merrily as I write. Fetch has a silk garter around his neck. The poodles wear ribbons tied to their tail stubs. I'm going to have erotic dreams if I ever get to sleep. They all reek of perfume, these lascivious bedmates. I don't know if I like the Boomie people loving my dogs. But at least they didn't harm them.

The sounds I heard weren't gunshots or firecrackers. They were the lovecracks of whips. Boomie, being a fancier of amusing and pleasurable whippings, has many whip lovers among her fans, you see. That's what two of them were doing when I arrived: making love with whips. Their champions, a man and a woman they called Majority Whip and Minority Whip, were having congress across the campfire. I sat with the dogs, and we joined the others in cheering them on. Fascinating to watch their whips snake through the moonlight, lash out and flick against each other's bodies, nipping pleasure at the edge of pain. No wonder Boomie gives them such a thrill.

After the love contest was over, we got to examine their whips. His was the heaviest. It was equipped with a feathered French tickler. Hers only had a forked tongue of soft red leather. But she won. They had both love-cracked each other from head to toe and were resting in ecstasy, with their whips wriggling on the ground behind them, when she suddenly ran toward him, right up to the edge of the fire. Her whip streaked straight forward, caught his whip arm and brought it down against his body, then whirled around him, wrapped him up tight and, with one sudden tug, yanked him off the ground, over the flames, into her arms.

We cheered her victory wildly. The dogs barked like maniacs. Papouli doesn't like that kind of behavior. Being an advocate of cooperative entertainments, he doesn't approve of the emotions these competitions arouse.

Never mind. The moon's gone down. I feel for Papouli in his struggle to be good. He must be very apprehensive, but excited too. He's the one who has suffered the most since we lost his father. The number seven governs all aspects of cosmic evolution, and human evolution is united with that of the cosmos. If he thinks of a solution he'll be a much happier man, and he'll have Mamouli safely where he wants her. Look. He's still over there on the porch next to his gorilla. He must be getting somewhere. He just handed Dad another cigar. See how he fills his friend's glass with another shot of whiskey. A good omen. Purist that Papouli is, I often wonder how he'd hold out if he couldn't project his vices onto the ape.

Papouli stands, stretches, lays a hand on Dad's shoulder. Dad leans back in his chair, crosses a foot over his knee, throws back the whiskey in one gulp, thumps his shiny, black-armored chest and holds out his glass for more. Papouli reaches for the bottle on the railing and pours him yet another. Then he opens the screen door and goes inside, taking the bottle with him.

Dad should be staggering in as soon as he finishes this last one and smokes his cigar down to the ash. There he sits, calm as ever — indifferent, you might say. I think he must spend most of his time dreaming of a very distant land. You'd think a drunk, nostalgic gorilla would get violent or something. It's crude, I know, but I keep wondering what he does for the satisfaction of his sexual needs. He's looks like such a virile fellow. Anyhow, he's one character I don't have to worry about just now. He'll be lucky if he can stand up and get himself into bed between Bimbo and Bimba.

I haven't told you much about the twins, or about Polyphemus, but there's really not much I can say by way of characterization. Bimbo and Bimba remain a mystery to me. From the way they do magic, I thought they understood the *great* mysteries. But Polyphemus says no.

"Robert," our giant says, "the twins do not understand the mysteries. They represent them for us because they know them. To know the mysteries is to know that you don't understand them. The more you know, the less you understand. When Bimbo and Bimba know the mysteries entirely, they'll understand absolutely nothing."

He smiles euphorically when he says that. It's strange with Polyphemus. He's like the Great Grand-Papouli used to be. I can quote him at length without having the slightest idea what he's talking about. Papouli doesn't understand him either, though he always takes the giant's advice when we're in a fix; and Polyphemus is usually right. The brilliant idea that made Papouli stand up just now and go to bed with such satisfaction was probably the idea of asking Polyphemus what to do. All Papouli really does, I think, is generate the power that enables our rather sleepy giant to stay mentally awake. I know Polyphemus has been stretched out on his bed all this time with hands behind his head and third eye wide open. His night light has been on, too, in the wagon across the way. And see? It just went out. I hope he's thought up an act for our new man. It'll be nice to have some fresh excitement in our circus. What could the lad possibly do?

Ah, my loves! Just a brief prayer for Mamouli and I can lie down at last.

There's nothing like a panting perfumed poodle bed.

11

I'M SO EXCITED! Hot dog! (oops) Hooray! We're going to have a big party for Boomie's lover tonight! I can hardly wait! I took my turn looking at his face through Dad's binoculars this afternoon, from where we were all gathered in the Papouli wagon. I like his smile. It's sad, but pleasantly sad. Isn't sadness a kind of love? Love for something irretrievably lost? It's a pure emotion. "The lad's face is pure," Mamouli declared. "Whatever's left behind is left behind. A very, very, *very* good sign. And there's laughter in the eyes. Don't you think, Bobby? You have an eye for laughter."

"He has the clown eye," I said with confidence. "The fool's twinkle."

We kept snatching the binoculars away from one another to have another look. They were seated in the sunlight on the porch of Boomie's wagon, she in his blue shirt and Levi's, he in her red satin robe. If he can do for us what he's already done for Boomie, we'll be fine. I never saw her looking so relaxed; she leaned her head against his shoulder and grinned in that dreamy way which said, "So it's happened to me at last," while her watery eyes asked, "Why has it taken so long?"

Papouli said that Boomie was genuinely in love this time. "The fidget's gone out of her. Look. The energy's flowing downward. She's not just sitting there. She's *sitting* there." And we all laughed because just then she stood up and sat on the lad's shoulders. He carried her around the wagon three times while the birds flocked above them and she tousled his shaggy black hair. Then they went inside and shut the door, he and Boomie and all the birds.

Papouli said, "They're just like us, Mamouli." He hugged her and tried to kiss her, but she turned her face away and said, "Well, not exactly," and we chuckled because they'd just had one of their terrible fights.

"Kiss me, Mamouli. My passions have been stirred."

"By *her*. Not by me."

"What difference does it make? We're all the same, aren't we?"

"Oh, all right," and she kissed him on the chin and the cheeks and the forehead and the nose, and then Dad stepped up and took their heads in his hands and fixed them against each other mouth to mouth and grunted, and we watched our circus mother and father kiss for a good long time, and you could hear the sigh of relief.

• •

I should have known the wait was over when I picked up the little person in my car this morning. Little people always seem to appear in my life at times of transition. Things have to go really wrong, don't they, before there's any hope of their going right. They went worse than bad at last night's performance.

Annie wouldn't do her belly dance. She just wagged her rump insultingly at Papouli and sat down, threw her trunk around Mamouli's waist, pulled her to her bosom and kissed her on the neck right there in front of everybody. The Solomons climbed to the top of the masts when they were supposed to be down in the sawdust with me, aping my ape imitations. They just hung up there by one hand scratching their chins, while I practically had to blow my butt off trying to make up for the laughs they refused to get. And Dad: When you don't let a gorilla swing through the trees at least once a day, you have to expect him to get carried away. He threw Papouli clear out of the wrestling ring into the dolphin tank. Jill became the world's first unsmiling dolphin, Jack rolled over and played dead like Fetch, and Mamouli had to dive in and console them with a basket of fish before they'd dance on their tails. They refused to jump through the hoop. Mamouli had to do that while I held it and was nearly drowned by the waves. God! She comes out of the water like a whale in mating season! But that wasn't what the crowd paid for, and Mamouli sure hates to get booed.

Fetch wouldn't herd the sheep and the sheep started humping, which gave them away for the horny French poodles they really are. Calypso refused to open his jaws to let Polyphemus stick his head in. The cats wouldn't leap to their platforms. They just paced about the cage sniffing. When circus animals can't forget the feed greed long enough to perform, you might as well fold up the tent.

After the show, Papouli called all the animals into the elephant pavilion and chewed them out for half an hour — accused them of insubordination, and of organizing a virtual strike, and threatened to have Dad do a King Kong on them if they didn't shape up. But Dad sided with them. He jogged over to a corner, turned his back on Papouli, folded his arms across his chest and sat there sulking.

"Okay!" shouted Papouli. "You want me to let them go out and play. Go! Go, the whole pack of you! Scare hell out of everybody. Get lost in the dump. Eat garbage, I don't care." He kicked at the dirt. "You don't have to come back either. I'm canceling the show."

Elated, and not the least bit frightened by Papouli's tantrum, the animals tore out of the tent to go join the fun at Boomie's camp, where I'm sure some kind of orgy was going on by then, those exotics were all so restless.

• •

First thing in the morning, with the animals still out gallivanting, I drove into town to slap up cancel notices. That's when I saw the little person. He was walking along in the tall grass, barely visible on the other side of the ditch, and I thought at first he was an authentic pixy or troll, but then I recognized the bellhop uniform and knew it was our friend Beauty the Midget. Beauty used to sit on Polyphemus's lap in the old days when they were freaks together, before Beauty was hired by a cigarette company and made it big in TV commercials. After Beauty repented of that job, he went on the road to preach the little people's gospel. Our caravan often passed him, but he had said so many insulting things to Polyphemus about Poly's outrageous and immoral size that our giant wouldn't let us stop to give him a ride any more. Being alone, however, I stopped, threw open my door and called to Beauty to hop in.

"Howdy, Bob," he said in that transistor-radio voice of his, and the moment he was in the car he laid his pack down between us, patted it and started right in with his usual spiel. He said it was a lie what kids were told in school. The dinosaurs didn't become extinct. They just wised up and made themselves small. Only the dumb ones stayed big and died. The vast majority turned themselves into lizards. Beauty the Midget patted his pocket. Three happy chameleons popped up, hooked their claws over the edge, flicked their tongues and wagged their heads until the pocket's gold button, which hung below them by a loose thread, began to swing like a pendulum in time to the music the midget whistled.

"Nice act," I said.

"They got it made, Bob. Lay your hand on my pack."

I touched the top of the little cloth backpack and quickly withdrew my hand. "What kind of creature's wiggling around in there?" I asked. "Wouldn't be a rattlesnake, would it?"

"Nothing that big, Bob. It's not a single creature. It's something like three hundred of the darlings. Lizards they are. Little dinosaurs. And they're mighty comfortable too. Feeling right at home. I give them away to children to remind them to stay small and not grow up supermarket fat like their folks. Them lizards'll be living behind the ear, in the hair, in a pocket or a sock, and they'll feel just as comfortable as they do now. Here." He snatched one of the chameleons out of his pocket and stuck it in mine. "Have one. You couldn't have a better friend."

I took the lizard out and put it back in Beauty's pocket. "Can't," I said. "You know how Papouli has to approve any new animal that enters our act."

"Suit yourself. Only these ain't no ordinary animals. These little fellers have got the secret of redemption locked in their skin and stored in their glands. If you're looking for spiritual heroes, you need look no further."

I reminded Beauty of the time he shot the chameleon man in the leg, back at the big circus. The man had been walking about in the stands selling chameleons fastened to pins you could stick on your shirt. Shooting the man, I said, was an act of mercy, and I was glad Polyphemus had hidden Beauty in his hat.

Beauty blushed. "I have to admit, Poly saved my life. And he kept me from shooting the man in the other leg, because I would have, you know. Can't abide cruelty to lizards. They're us little people's little people. Taught us how to vanish, how to roll our eyes."

"Are you a bona fide dues-paying little person now?" I asked, teasing him because I knew he wasn't. He could roll his eyes, but he couldn't vanish. That was his sorrow. His imperfection.

"Not exactly. But I seen them, Bob. I crossed over and explored their home territory and I seen them. They don't really vanish, you know. They just adapt their colors to whatever's standing behind them. You should tell that to Mamouli. If she still wants to vanish from the ground so bad, tell her she doesn't have to step up off of it. All she has to do is take on the local color. Stand in front of a tree and look like a tree. If the tree moves, become a rock, if the rock rolls away, become a hill. If the hill moves, to hell with it. Then you can walk on air, but not before. It's not worth all the trouble. Here." He pulled the top string of his green canvas pack and opened it wide. "See anything?"

I glanced inside. "Looks empty to me."

"But your hand felt them, Bob, so you know they're in there. Ain't it more than clever?"

"It's the secret of the universe, no doubt about that. Can *you* make yourself invisible, Beauty? Now that you've seen them and talked to them?"

"Alas and alack, they got mad at me and vanished into a giant cabbage. I suppose I outspoke myself regarding that big, dumb vegetable. I told them they were crazy to brag on how they'd helped the cabbage grow. 'Shrink it down,' I said. They didn't take to that. Said they'd just as soon get their advice from the man. 'The man?' I says. 'Have you forgot the lizard who taught you?' That's when they vanished. I did learn this much, though. They not only know how to change the color of their skins. They know how to change the color of their clothes. That's what makes them so human. When I've preached my message to the people, I'm going back to the old country with a good conscience and I'm going to get in for keeps with the little people. We midgets are tired of being the lost tribe. Are you ready for some preaching, Bob?"

"All ears," I said.

He put the pack on his lap and slid over closer to me. "We've got to make ourselves small, Bob. That's the essence."

"I know we do, Beauty."

71

"No more huge heroes. Put the lid on the Super Bowl."

"It's going to be a hard message to take. No more Polyphemus, Beauty?"

"Not if we can help it. Sterilize the big ones, I say. Only let the tiniest people on the planet reproduce. Phase out the ten-ton football players. Stop cheering the basketball behemoths."

"The behemoths are bad, Beauty?"

"*We're* bad to look up to them with such awe. Big is bad, Bob. You'd do well to tell Mamouli and that elephant of hers to stop eating so much. They take up an unconscionable amount of room. It takes too many leaves to work up all the air they breathe. This car we're in is too big, Bob. For fie! Don't look to the right. We're passing the Big Orange. Can't they see we gotta reduce? With our knowledge of chemistry, I estimate we could have people down to the size of toy soldiers in ten generations and still get plenty of muscle from the machine. A whole city could live in a single room. A family in a dresser drawer. The U.N. secretary general is going to let me make a speech about it. We could use a real Pygmy in that post, you know. I'll explain how the little people were giants once. They just wised up, like the dinosaurs."

"You're spreading a valuable message," I said.

"I offend people. I know I do. But truth will out. The truth is, you have to take the *great* out of your circus, buddy. It's too much. Call yourselves The Papouli Circus or The Little Papouli Circus. The Little Mamouli, the Little Papouli, Bimbina and Bambino, get it? Tell the twins to work on a shrinkage machine. With their technical know-how, they could send us to the stars in a ship the size of a thimble, with no waste of fuel. For the love of St. Thomas Thumb, Bob, we can make computers right now so small you have to have another computer to find where they're at. And they can still commit more of a nuisance than they should. It's time to be tiny. Let's make that our slogan. Don't you agree?"

I stopped the car in front of the YMCA. He shook my finger and slid out the door, dragging his pack of lizards after him. "I agree," I said. I hurried on to levitation class feeling so inspired that I was hardly seated with the others when, shrunk down in my mind's eye to the size of a dust particle, I was lifted easily off the mat. I drifted about in total euphoria during the entire class and landed so gently you wouldn't even have known I'd finally done it. (Or had I?)

• •

I hurried up the steps of the Papouli wagon as soon as I got back, so elated that I had already opened the screen door before I remembered I'd forgotten to post the cancellation notices. Mamouli and Papouli were into such a shouting match that I was afraid to add to their fire, so I just dumped myself into a chair to rest and listen before driving back to town.

Mamouli must have thrashed about in one of her doomsday dreams last night. The sheets were on the floor. Over the bed, the votive candle on the altar to the Virgin had been blown out. The room smelled of burned food (Mamouli only burns food to punish Papouli's stomach). Dad was squatting none too steadily in the window seat, looking in the direction of Boomie's wagon

73

through a pair of binoculars. He reminded me of a cartoon I once saw, where an old man with a telescope peers out through his curtain at the window across the street and says, "Has that woman no shame?"

While they argued, Mamouli massaged Papouli's neck, trying to release the tension even as it was being created. He was seated astraddle a kitchen chair with her behind him, his head pulled back almost violently into the softness of her stomach. In Mamouli's eyes, I saw the temptation if not to strangle him at least to prevent him from speaking. She was at work on his larynx, just below the Adam's apple. He's been having trouble down there from all the lighter fluid that's seared his throat during so many years of swallowing fire.

"The world's not coming to an end," Papouli said. "That's ridiculous. Just because we have a little crisis."

"A *little* crisis," Mamouli scoffed. "The whole world's in collision. How much larger can a crisis get? This planet's practically come to a stop."

"Everytime we come to a stop, you think the whole world stops with us. Tell me, sweetheart, how many more years do you give yourself to live?"'

"Me personally? Thirty, maybe forty."

"And how much longer do you give the world?"

"About the same."

"Isn't that the way it always is. So great is the human ego that we just can't believe the world is going to get along without us. When we have our judgment day, everybody else has to have it too. When we go down, the world goes down with us — that's what apocalyptic visions are all about. They're our own demise projected onto the entire planet. You don't believe the world's coming to an end, do you, kids?"

74

"I don't," said Bimba.

"Nor I," said Bimbo.

"See? I hate to tell you this, sweetheart, but the human race is going to leave this planet in its own jolly good time, without being rushed by a bunch of seventh-day self-centered religious fanatics!"

"Watch your words," said Mamouli. "And don't call me sweetheart when you talk like that. In fact, don't call me anything. I'll call you."

"Not when you keep wanting to get off the line."

Mamouli's thumbs dug in hard. "Listen to me, you big blowhard. I have eyes. I have a nose. Earth's dying. She's mucked. Her veins are clogged, her pores can't breathe, her breath stinks. Go take another walk in that garbage dump they made us pitch our tent by. Your father would have had a fit even in his dreams, just from the stench of all that petrochemical crap they're trying to burn. Strips of plastic have drifted up and snagged on the flagpole. Isn't that right, Bobby?"

"If everybody in the world would just put on overalls," I said. "Pick up rake, shovel or hoe. We're meant to be caretakers of this planet. The rest is pure mischief."

"Last month when we camped on the beach," Mamouli continued, "plastic bags covered the sand as far as the eye could see. You were afraid to swim because of all the jellyfish, until I showed you they were just more plastic bags. How can you say we haven't smothered the earth? She's gasping."

"It's not that bad," Papouli said. "You're in this mood because the animals scared the Boomie aficionados away. They'll be back. They're just hiding in the woods for a while. Did you get the show canceled, Bobby?"

75

"I forgot," I said. "I'll drive back shortly."

"You drove all the way into town and you forgot? Great God! What were you doing? Jerking yourself off again at the — "

Mamouli's thumbs dug harder at his throat and cut off his voice before he could give away the secret I didn't want her to know. She turned to me with a mean grin. "See, Robert? A still small voice has been silenced in the land." Papouli's eyes were popping. His feet kicked out. She clenched her teeth. Her hands tightened like a vice. "Nothing to say."

Papouli reached back and grabbed her wrists, but let us not deceive ourselves. Papouli might be able to lift an elephant on his back, but Mamouli was the one who bent the bars of Dad's cage when they spirited him away from the zoo. "Mute," she said. "Squelched by the power of truth."

Papouli smiled despite himself. He dropped his arms and went limp. Mamouli relaxed her grip, brought her big mitts around now gently to his neck and shoulders, began to knead in that expert way of hers, the way she works the dough for our bread every morning. Papouli groaned with pleasure. "Ah, yeah, that feels good. Look, loves, I have it all figured out. This young man may be just what we need to give our circus the lift we've longed for, to really get us off the ground."

Mamouli, who had her own idea of how to get us off the ground, hid her hurt again.

I said, "We knew you'd come up with something. Have you decided to ask Polyphemus?"

"That's not coming up with something, smart-ass. I don't need Big Third-Eye to tell me about the seventh chakra. I've had more out-of-the-body experiences than he's ever had. Polyphemus is an important part of us, but he has the mentality of a Newton, and if there's anything we've learned during the last few centuries it's that Newton was half right, which means he was also half wrong, which means he came up with exactly nothing. Newton suffered from gravity. The grave. Death was his subject. His bright idea was to put everything down in the dark. And he had the nerve to call his the age of enlightenment."

"Have you ever read Newton, Papouli?" Bimba asked.

"I don't have to read him. His perverse influence makes itself felt wherever life becomes a drag. We're only now coming out of the shadow of his so-called bright idea."

Dad put down his binoculars and shot a mean glance at Papouli. Papouli had spoken often enough about Dad's role as his shadow. Dad did not like being called a shadow, and he had picked the word out as pertaining to him. He reached for an apple on the sideboard, took one menacing chomp of it and threw it at Papouli's feet. Then he put the binoculars to his eyes again, bent forward, adjusted them and peered out even more intently than before.

"Gravity through levity," Papouli declared, "that's the secret Dad and Newton both fail to understand. People like Newton, who arrive at ideas through the brain, without exercising the body, always stay underneath what they think they're on top of. Newton just sat under his tree and sulked, waiting for a revelation. He got it."

"The apple hit the floor," I said with a wink toward Dad.

"You've hit it on the head, Bobby."

"Eureka!" said I.

"We at The Great Papouli Circus *perform* our perceptions. We follow through, Bobby boy. With us, gravity not only leads to the apple, but the apple leads to the fall, and the fall leads directly to what? Quick! To what?"

"Give me a hint."

"What goes up must come what, Bobby?"

"Down," says I.

"Down," says he. "But what Sir Isaac failed to understand correctly is that whatever comes down must also come . . ."

"Up!" cry I.

"Bravo! Take your bow. Which leads us to whom?"

"Personally," said Mamouli, "I never gave a fig for Newton."

"Then put the cookie back in the box and stay out of this," Papouli said, "unless you know how to think it through. Who always gets it up when it comes down?"

"Okay," muttered Mamouli. "Boomie gets it up for men. So what?"

"So now! The apple leads to the fall and the fall leads to whom, my friend?"

"The apple," say I, "leads to Adam."

"Superb! Bobby, your mind is a storage vault of the same old deductions. But I mean — "

"It leads to Boomie," I exclaim, catching on at last.

"It leads to Boomie's new man, our new performer, who was down in the ditch in the dumps, in a slump, and who's now, through her expertise, learning how to get it up again, which gives us a clue to the solution of our problem. Down he goes and then up he goes." Papouli stood, spread out his arms. I imitated a drumroll with my tongue. I blew a trumpet fanfare through my lips. I put my finger to my cheek and thumped the bass drum.

"Ladeeze and gentlemen, boys and girls," cried Papouli so loudly that Dad threw the binoculars aside to cover his ears. "The Great Papouli Circus is happy to present its latest and greatest attraction. The Grrrrreatest Fall on Earth!"

I didn't know just what he had in mind, and it seemed to me he better talk to Polyphemus, but his enthusiasm sounded promising, and I applauded wildly.

Papouli snatched up the binoculars, fixed them to his eyes and suddenly leaned toward the window. "What's this? My God, Dad, why didn't you say something? They're out of the wagon. They're sitting on the front step necking. Bobby, you're a genius at forgetting. Now we can still put on the show. Round up the animals, we've got to get ready. Let's be terrific tonight!"

Mamouli seized the binoculars from him and beamed at what she saw. Then I looked at the couple across the field on the silver steps, and, hearing our excitement, Polyphemus and the Solomons hurried over to have a look-see.

"After the show, we'll have a feast!" cried Papouli. "We'll bring out the wine and put on the shine. We don't want to look like some two-bit tank-town carnival. We'll light the candles, lay out the linen, dress in our finery, show him our stuff. Where's my fluff-collar shirt? Did you iron it, Mamouli? Christ, give me those binoculars! Let's have another look at this guy!"

12 ✤

LET ME REPORT the good news immediately. We've all taken an immense liking to Boomie's lover, and I think he's taken an equal liking to us. In fact, he acts as if he's known us and loved us for a long time. Every funny little thing we do delights him.

Don't ask me his name. Boomie won't tell us. She says we have to guess. None of us has the slightest idea who he is, yet she says every one of us has met him and entertained him. "You mean he's one of our fans?" asked Bimba. "We met him when he was in the stands, you mean," said Bimbo. This made Boomie's lover laugh.

"Not in the stands," he said. "In the — "

"Hush!" Boomie teased. "We'll give you one last hint. He's one of us." Then she added, pleased with herself, "He's a member of the mystical circus."

"One of the Incredible Flying Farfans," declared Papouli. "I didn't recognize you. You've grown up, Tato."

Our mysterious friend thrust his hands into his pockets and leaned back with a twinkle in his eye. "I've never been in a circus tent in my life. The only circus I've ever seen was in a movie starring Burt Lancaster and Gina Lollobrigida."

"And you're a member of the mystical circus," said Polyphemus. "I begin to understand."

"Then tell us," I said.

"I've *begun* to understand, Robert. I haven't finished."

"Strike up the music, Bobby," Papouli said. "Let's dance. We'll have our good friend figured out before the night's ended. I never forget a face." He seized Mamouli by the waist. I whipped my harmonica out of my pocket and blew "The Beer Barrel Polka," and one terrific party got under way, because when circus people get high I mean they get high. We danced on the roofs of the wagons, jumped over the moon, flung food across the table into each other's mouths, ran about balanced on our hands kicking a ball, tumbled on the tablecloth, blew out the candles at ten paces and blew fire at them to light them again. What a bunch of showoffs! Well, he didn't hang back from the rest of us. He was plainly where he wanted to be, as if he had come home at last. Mamouli almost ate him up. Once she starts feeding and fussing over someone, you know their wanderings are likely to be over for a good long time.

I'm writing this at high noon with a hangover. Headachy but happy. Our camp is still asnore. What shall I report of our blue-eyed, black-haired friend?

That Boomie chose someone sensible for a change. A beautiful and modest youth, attentive, not given to talk but gentle and kind when he speaks. There is such humor in his sadness that I don't know whether to call it sadness at all. His wide, full-lipped mouth, with its youthful wisps of mustache, is downturned, so that he does look mournful as he approaches, but the wit of his eyes so mocks his suffering that you might say the eyes transform the mouth into its opposite. The mouth suffers and the eyes forgive. I love ambiguity. Papouli says that without strong opposites in your character it's impossible to get your act off the ground. A good performer has to be saturated in irony. When the act reaches its peak, you should never be quite sure whether you're laughing or weeping. Boomie's lover does the funniest things with the grimmest expression, then goes off by himself to stand by one of the animals, with a smile so melancholy that you rush over to console him with a glass of wine and a cheerful word. From behind his back a glass of wine appears, he clicks the glass that you've extended, says "*L'chaim!*" then pats you on the back while you're bent over laughing and asks ever so tenderly, "You okay? You sick?"

I love him.

You should see Mamouli. She couldn't stop picking him up and whirling him around. Finally he somehow got up on her shoulders, with a stray chicken squawking on his head, and played an imaginary fiddle. Papouli sidled over to me. "I think I've got it, Bobby. What do they look like right now?"

"I was thinking a painting by Chagall."

"Here's a hint. The impulse to leap. Unreasonable conduct. Got it?"

"Suzuki, the Sudden Flash."

"He passed on ten years ago. Try again. Who have you

heard of lately who has that same recklessness welling up from the heart? Come on, Bobby."

"Not Harry Hassid, the Flying Rabbi?"

"The same."

"But he's a myth."

"Myths live."

Though he'd guessed wrong, thinking he'd guessed right put Papouli in such a good mood he didn't even make his usual scene when Mamouli announced she was going to walk on air. As Mamouli crouched on the table, hesitant, casting her pleading glance at Papouli, our chief just folded his arms over his stomach and shrugged. Our new friend felt that bit of tension and released it immediately by jumping right up there with Mamouli. Both gave a whoop and took off at once. Mamouli crashed right down, but he — my goodness! — he managed to stay up for a little while, I swear, pedaling his feet in the air, flapping his hands, his tongue stuck out wiggling; and when he fell he still found time to flatten his body and belly flop right on top of Mamouli, who, to our amazement, was the first to roar with laughter, seizing the lad in her huge arms and hugging him for dear life while he, sad-faced as ever, kicking his legs, sounded a perfect cry of birth, curled up in her lap in a fetal position, and, with an audacity we couldn't help but admire, pulled down Mamouli's blouse and greedily fastened his mouth to her nipple. It was impossible not to scream with delight, because he had caught on so quickly to what pleasured her. Mrs. Solomon sprang up chattering and pointing and finally rolled in a ball along the ground in such frenzy that we had to run after her, catch her and carry her home, where Mr. Solomon put her to bed and crawled in next to her, petting her ardently in a touching attempt to calm the seizure. Animals have such a perpetual longing for joy that when it breaks out excessively in humans it's sometimes more than they can take. They were in rapture over Boomie's lover, almost pathetically grateful for what he'd released in us.

When lions want to lick your face and dogs jump into your arms, when chimps go home sick with excitement and a gorilla offers you his last genuine Cuban cigar, you know something healthy is going on.

"Harry, you're terrific," Papouli said to him.

"My name's not Harry. Guess again."

"A small hint."

"You saved my life."

"Saved your life?"

"Saved my life. You and Bob and Boomie, Mamouli, Polyphemus, Bimbo and Bimba."

Papouli held our friend at arms' distance and looked at him long and hard. He shook his head. "But you never saw us perform."

"Not in the tent."

Then the lad did something that somehow nobody else would presume to do. He took hold of Papouli by the ears. Reached right under his thick golden mane and grabbed him, kissed him on his Santa Claus nose.

Papouli blinked. Then he, too, got strangely carried away. He pulled the lad into his arms and almost seemed to be sobbing as he said, "It's a great relief to have you with us. It's the life of this family I think you've come to save."

The lad laughed good-naturedly. The two men stepped

back again and looked at each other with a kind of fierce appreciation. "You'll begin by just playing the fool. Bob can teach you how. Just try out whatever feels right. Then you can start learning how to fall."

We had all gathered around, and when he said, "Whatever you say, Papouli," we cheered and took turns embracing him. Boomie pretended to be jealous and began to belly dance to get his attention. That's when he proved to be every bit the one-man band that I am. He started blowing a burlesque trumpet, with his lips puckered just right. I faked the bass fiddle, flicking my fingers against my cheeks. Simultaneously I sang clarinet. Polyphemus beat the drum on his top hat and we got so much music going that even the animals were dancing on air.

Boomie's aficionados heard us on the wind. They approached cautiously. When Dad saw them, he walked over and invited them so politely to join us that they lost their fear. They came swarming over. What a party! In the midst of it all I became a bit panicky, as I always do when things get manic. Those gaudy, sexy, earringed men with their cocks tight in their pants were all over Boomie. They grabbed her and passed her around, petted and kissed her and God knows what else. I was sure the new member of our family was going to explode, but he saw how Boomie was enjoying herself so he just lay back and let it happen. I was the one who couldn't take it. I went over to the corral fence and stood in the dark with Polyphemus, who had busted the top of his hat and was using this as an excuse to look glum, though I knew he was as uneasy about Boomie as I was.

"She's testing him," I said. "She's giving him the big

jealousy test. What if he doesn't pass? What'll she do to herself if she drives him away?"

"She has to have him on her own terms, Robert. That's the way she is."

"I can't stand this flirting with self-destruction."

"Yes, you can. That's why you're in the circus."

"Okay," I said. "But you can read his mind, can't you? Give me a clue. Who is he? Does he really want to be in the circus? Does he have the courage?"

"You know very well I don't read minds. I only pretend to read minds. I read feelings, Robert, and those are what you're asking me about."

(It's true. Polyphemus is as much of a fake as the rest of us. We don't really do what we appear to do, though the illusions we create are even more fantastic. If people knew what we really did, it would blow their minds. Most of us learned our skills from the animals. Polyphemus learned his from our horse Pegasus. Ask Pegasus how much seven and seven is and he'll start striking the ground with his hoof, right? That horse doesn't know how to count. It's all fake. What he does is watch the crowd. When he reaches fourteen, he sees a hysterical flow of excitement ripple across their faces. Everybody may think they're keeping absolutely poker-faced, but horses are infinitely more sensitive to muscular change than we are, just as dogs are more sensitive to smell. A horse communicates with his own species by rippling his skin. According to Polyphemus, who spent years in the fields studying their conversation, horses have an acutely poetic skin vocabulary. The subject of horse conversation mostly has to do with wind and motion, with catching the flow of waves across the grasses, with glints on stones and qualities of earth and cloud and smoke and the horrors of fire. Horse love speaks of shudder, twist, tailtease, mount and thrust; its whinny is the mere exhalation of excess language, the linguistic residue of aroused flesh.)

So I told Polyphemus, "I don't care how you read. Just give me the information." We were standing at the outskirts of the party, while Boomie belly danced for her devotees, her hair brushing their faces as they stood in a circle, jiving with their hips and wiggling braceleted hands.

"I wish I could have a look at him with his clothes off," he said. "I'd like to read his belly and balls. I'd like to study his rump. But so far I'd say he's for staying."

"Great. You've set my mind at rest."

"I don't deal with the mind, Bob. I *am* the mind," he said in that impatient tone I have never particularly liked. Polyphemus is at the other end of things from me. I respond to him as I do to mathematicians, composers and computers — with a slight chill. He can never be reassuring without immediately reversing himself.

"I deal with feelings," he said, "and I must warn you that I'll be greatly surprised if our friend still feels like staying, after he finds out what Papouli really has in store for him."

"Hasn't Papouli told him?"

"My Humpty-Dumpty plan? Not really."

"Why not?"

"Because I haven't told Papouli yet. I want to wait until we see how good he is at just fooling around and falling."

"Will you tell me?"

"Tell you?" Polyphemus chuckled in deep bass tones of ultimate masculine mockery. "Good grief."

I left the party at that point and went to sulk in my wagon. I'm not the gossip everybody thinks I am. I keep this journal hidden under my mattress. I get depressed when people think I'm some kind of hysterical clown, just because I play that part in the tent. Hell, I'm the foundation of this show. I'm its rock.

Anyhow, my optimism has returned with the morn. Or is it afternoon? Papouli's out there doing his Tai Chi. How could a big man move with such grace if he didn't have everything under control? Papouli's the boss of this outfit, after all. Polyphemus is nothing but a mental gymnast working to keep suspense in the air. My confidence is absolute. Yes it is. It definitely is. I am brimming. But what's that!?

Papouli just clapped his hands and let out a whoop. He's pointing toward Boomie's wagon. Hold on a sec.

• •

Why didn't I recognize him first? I never recognize anything first. My God, this is wonderful news! Guess who Boomie's taken up with? We *did* save his life. I'm the one who figured out how. Bob the Grip, you son of a burlesque comedian and a small-town tap-dance teacher, if it hadn't been for you he wouldn't even be with us! Let me take *you* by the ears and kiss *you* on both cheeks, you darling man! You've delivered to our door none other than the Great Lazarus!

13 ✎

I'D LIKE TO TELL YOU right away the story of the Great Lazarus and how we saved his life. But, since it was the evil eye of Mrs. Poindexter that almost did him in, I feel that I must explain who this woman was, so as not to besmirch the reputation of one of the great originals in the line of mystical entertainers.

• •

After you've traveled the roads of this land as much as we have, you get so you can't stand the sight of chains — food chains, motel chains, theater chains. Chains. You get to detest them just as much as the animals do. Imagine a chain of Great Papouli Circuses. People in this land must be getting mighty insecure, to count so much on coming upon exactly what they came upon in the town before. Folks who start something original by way of food, lodging or entertainment hardly stand a chance. If the chains adhered to a genuine tradition, it would be different. But the places that call themselves inns, for example, don't even have a place where you can sit and swap stories by the fire or tell what kind of pilgrimage you're on. The Mrs. Poindexter's Tea Houses you see at the edge of town don't have the slightest notion of the wonderful woman whose method they presume to perpetuate.

Mrs. Poindexter was a real master of the tea ceremony. She studied in Japan during the war, when she was a WAC, and returned to found the justly famous Poindexter approach to tea reading, which, I'm sorry to say, has been corrupted beyond recognition today. The rickety house is prefabricated in Grand Rapids; the busted sign with the picture of the yellow tea pot that swings sideways in the wind, on one hinge, is stamped out of a mold in Guadalajara and shipped to the Mrs. Poindexter Main Office in Tulsa. The teapots, cups and saucers say on the bottom that they're made in Korea, but they're actually made in Cuba. The originals were made of bone china and passed on through three generations with loving care. The tea readers graduate from the Poindexter Tea Academy after only two weeks' training. It's a disgrace.

All of us at the circus went to the original Mrs. Poindexter at one time or another to have our tea leaves read. Her broken-down old woodslat house, with its front yard overrun with weeds and a few dozen cats asleep on the sagging porch and the broken sign hanging from a tree near the road, always tempted us to pull over so one of us could go through the ritual and report back with the inevitable news of good things to come.

You had to approach the gate alone or the dog would

drive you off. In any case, he'd rush at you barking furiously the moment he heard the rusty hinge creak. Today, the dog's just a hunk of plastic with a voice box, fixed in one spot on the lawn; but in those days a real dog attacked, and if you stood perfectly still and let him sniff you up and down while he kind of ripped at your socks with his fangs, he'd grudgingly let you pass. You approached the house. The cats scattered. You stepped carefully onto the porch, choosing the slats that looked solid. You knocked. Receiving no answer, you knocked again, waited, and then knocked really hard. A voice from inside demanded to know, "Whadya want!" You shouted that you'd come to have your tea leaves read.

She'd shout back that she wasn't in a mood, so go away. You stood there for a time, then you knocked again and insisted it was urgent. "Well, then, wait a minute," she'd grouch. And if you were a man she'd add, "Don't get your balls in an uproar, sonny. I'll have to put something on."

(For those of you who have been to a Mrs. Poindexter's Tea House and heard these words, I can assure you there isn't one practitioner who sounds even vaguely as cross and crabby as the original. For one thing, "Hold your pants on" just doesn't have the same tang.)

Imagine the scene. The door opens a crack, a scabby red eye looks you over, slips the chain and opens the door. You stand there watching an old woman in frayed bedroom slippers and some kind of soiled house smock walk away from you, favoring a bad hip. "Well, don't just stand there like a stump," she says. "Come in if you must. You'll have to sit back here in the kitchen. I'm in no mood to do no fancy entertaining."

Assaulted by the smell of cat piss, you pass through a living room littered with every kind of cheap magazine on the occult, into a not-too-clean kitchen, where you sit at a linoleum-covered table. Potato plants stuck with toothpicks, not plastic ivy vines, are growing out of Mason jars along the window sills. You admire them while she putters about getting the tea ready. Suddenly she turns on you, pulling down the lid of her left eye with a jaundiced finger, so you can see the red rim underneath and the yellowed white. "See this! The evil eye. That's right, sonny. You might as well know ahead of time, I seem to be cursed lately with the evil eye. Don't know how I got it or what it means. Alls I can tell you is, I haven't read a good fortune in the leaves since the last tornado hit ten years ago. That's why hardly nobody in their right mind comes to see me no more. I'd advise you to pick yourself up right now and skeedaddle, and no offense took. Faretheewell."

Ignoring this, you reach for your wallet and slap ten dollars down on the table. She snatches it up. "Tough, sonny," she says. "You had your chance. Now I'm hired. Got to feed my cats, you know. But don't expect me to see the best. I can't say whether it's the times going rotten or just this eye of mine, but I don't seem to ever see nothing but the very worst. Anyhow —" she shrugs; "Let's have a look, and don't hold it against me."

She pours the boiling water into the pot and sits across from you while she waits for the tea to steep. "Let's see that hand of yours." She grabs it and peers down with increasing dismay. "Land sakes, where's the life line? And ain't you got no heart?"

(Now, when they say that, you just laugh. But in those

days, you were struck with a genuine sense of foreboding and you behaved yourself.)

She tosses your hand aside. "Never mind. It's the tea that tells. Though from the looks of your hand and your face and the curl of your ears I gotta warn you, sonny, you look like the worst kind of loser to me. Drink your tea before it gets cold. I'm out of sugar and the cream's for my cats."

She pours with palsied hand, peering at you all the while with that evil eye, while half the tea slops into the saucer and across the slanted table and is sopped up neatly by a true-confession magazine. "Nope. Don't expect we're going to find much at the bottom by way of good news, but give me a look now." You take a last gulp of tea.

She pulls your cup close to her scrawny breast, sets her pointy chin down on her ribs and peers into the dregs. She looks up at you with disgust and then back at the tea leaves. "Must be some mistake. Let me go get my specs." She hobbles off, comes back wearing a thick pair of granny glasses, and stares wide-eyed into your cup again. She says that what she sees just doesn't make sense. "But the tea leaves never lie," she grumbles. "You sure as shootin' don't look the type, is all I can say. According to these here leaves, you're in for a huge heap of good fortune, goldarn it all. Sure beats me."

She then predicts the most wonderful future you could ever dream of. And the thing is, she doesn't just come off with some promise of love and wealth learned by rote, the way the Mrs. Poindexters do now. She knows how to draw the genuine daydreams out of the leaves. She told me I'd have as many dogs some day as she had cats, and I'd love them all and they'd love me and I'd end up becoming a custodian in the Garden of Eden. She had me dead to rights on that dream, and part of it came true. See? As for Mamouli, she told her she'd be so happy she'd be walking on air some day. Isn't that prediction close to fulfillment? Papouli was the only one who didn't like his fortune. She told him he'd end up looking at the sky so much that people would mistake him for a saint. *Mistake* him. That's the part that made him call her a purveyor of false hopes and dangerous illusions and all the rest; his reading ended in a shouting match on her front porch, with the seat of his trousers bitten out by the dog. But the rest of us have always loved to remember the readings of the great, original Mrs. Poindexter.

The women who work for the chain now wear premussed sloppy old-lady costumes with grease stains printed into the fabric. They sound grouchy in a funny way you catch onto right away as a gag. They're mostly young girls made up to look haggard, and they give you prefabricated happy readings and tell you afterward to clear out now and leave them in peace so they and the cats can have their nap and not be bothered with all this nonsense, then don't even take their naps but move right on to the next customer waiting by the gate for the plastic dog to bark.

Now you'll understand how one of these pseudo, mass-produced Mrs. Poindexters, fresh from her training in Tulsa, was responsible for the plight of Lazarus and for our having to save his life. I'll be ready to tell the story next break I get for writing.

14 🏵

YES, I'M PROUD TO SAY, it was none other than yours truly who made Lazarus laugh and, by so doing, unwittingly brought another clown into our ranks. I, Bob the Grip, saved our circus with my funny face, and I didn't even know it at the time.

We at The Great Papouli Circus only knew Lazarus by reputation then. No one else on the mystical circuit worked solo. His very name evoked an awesome solitude, an abysmal loneliness. We had heard rumors that he descended from a revered tradition of professional Christs, who were crucified every Good Friday in villages throughout Latin America; this practice having been banned about ten years ago, he left his family to try out a new act in our country — namely, being buried alive.

His was known as a good act to follow. You never pitched your tent while he was still performing, because he put folks on such a downer (ho ho). But after he had been raised from the ground and sent on his way the people were always eager for uplifting entertainment, and our show was just the ticket.

We never purposely pulled into town until we knew he was already off being buried farther up the pike. Once, on the dark of the moon, we arrived too early. He was still deep in the cold, cold ground of the city park. The universal gloom affected us so badly we weren't even in the mood to have a look at him in his casket; and that night something horrible happened to us that I'd just as soon not write about, for Mamouli's sake, except to say that we pulled up stakes and moved on.

The Great Lazarus filled a need people seem to have for ritual sacrifice. Perhaps in the past we knew how to suffer for our own redemption, but in this age of specialization we seem to have found it more convenient simply to hire someone to do the suffering for us. If a new civic building was to be raised, Lazarus was invited —at a good price — to be buried in the public park; a lighted air shaft was fitted through the ground to a hole in his casket, through which spectators who paid a certain amount could stare down at his face for fifteen seconds. He always took a vow to remain buried until the people who came to see him had paid out enough money to raise their school or hospital or civic center. Today there are buildings in every state of the union raised by the burial of Lazarus.

He usually arrived in town about a week ahead of time. The sweetness and modesty of his presence, plus his extreme good looks, caused children to adore him and young girls to fall in love with him and women to worship him and men to regard him with grim respect, so that he seldom had to stay in the ground more than three days and nights before the necessary funds had poured in. While he was in his casket he could raise his head to sip from a bag of water, but he would accept no food and he boasted that he could fast for forty days, though in truth (he told us) he had never gone without food before for more than ten days.

Then came the time when his act was severely tested.

On a certain Sunday in one of the villages off the great highway, the people were gathered in the public park for a picnic around the grave of the Great Lazarus. They lay sadly on the grass, in the sun, and every now and again went to pay another donation for one more look at the mysterious face of their hero. Amongst the crowd, dressed in a brand new old rag and bedroom slippers, was a fresh young graduate of the Poindexter Tea Academy, disguised as the famous old fortune-telling hag and eager to try out her new role. Just the day before, the company had delivered her rickety new Tea House, lifted it off the truck and installed it in a well-weeded yard next to Hamburger Heaven in the suburban shopping mall, and she was in town to see if she could roust up some business by insulting passers-by and otherwise behaving in the humorously surly way that every Mrs. Poindexter was famous for. While muttering dire predictions, snapping at children and complaining about the perfectly beautiful weather, she took her turn in line for a look at the man in the casket. When she stepped away from the shaft (I am reconstructing all this from evidence we gathered later), she pulled down her left eyelid and announced in a loud voice, "Beware the evil eye."

She was referring to her own eye, of course, but people

weren't that familiar with the Poindexter act yet, and they took her to mean that the evil eye belonged to the Great Lazarus. After she had hobbled off to her Tea House, word spread quickly among these superstitious people that Lazarus could put a curse on you if you looked down on him. This from no less authority than the famous syndicated tea-leaf reader herself.

The line grew shorter and shorter until, finally, there was no line at all — just an occasional civic official looking down to tell Lazarus not to panic. The hospital he was to help raise was very badly needed, and they were sure the public mood would change well before the end of the forty days he had agreed in his contract he would stay in the ground if necessary. They would certainly lower him food on the sly if need be. Professional pride got the better of Lazarus, however, and he said that he had always kept his part of the bargain. He would fast and, if need be, die, rather than be raised in forty, fifty or a hundred days without feeling the love of the people. They must willingly and gladly pay to look him in the eye. In fact, if he were dug up unfairly, he would sue the city for breach of contract and for destroying his reputation.

For the first time in his career, Lazarus found himself looking up at the sky and the stars. For days and nights on end not a single face looked down on him. The smiling faces that had always presented themselves to him, full of pity and encouragement, seen like beads in a rosary between little breaks of skylight, were sorely missed. They had become like a mantra to him. As each face appeared for its alloted fifteen seconds, he would try to see God's bright idea of that person while saying to himself, "The kingdom of heaven is within you." The joy of lying down there awakening expressions of perfect love with his vision was gone, replaced by an increasing sorrow as he grew weaker. His thoughts grew morbid. When he closed his eyes, his soul seemed to rush out of his body into icy subterranean rivers that tossed him about and brought him back to consciousness gagging for breath.

By the time Mrs. Poindexter's mistaken remark had been clarified, the people who finally ventured to look down saw a face so filled with horror, eyes so glazed by the kiss of death, that it seemed he did indeed have an evil leer, and they would not pay to have a second look.

We first found out about this when we read in the newspaper about a legal battle being fought between that town's government and its hospital officials, in league with Lazarus's booking agent, over whether a professional sufferer has the right to fast in public beyond a period of reasonable safety. Lazarus had been in the ground then, I believe, for thirty-two days. We decided to go to the rescue of our brother performer.

Once we had arrived at the grave, we looked down and saw that Lazarus didn't even appear to be conscious any more, and we realized that he was in even worse shape than we had imagined. He would very soon have to be dug up — in which case his career would be ended — or we would have to think up some clever way to rally the people back to the grave. That's when I had my bright idea. Actually, it was Boomie's to start with. The rest of us set up our mirrors and opened our makeup kits right there in the park, and we painted funny faces while she began to seduce Lazarus awake.

Boomie's is a silent act, and she's seldom given to speech, but her every aspect is sexy, including one hell of a sultry voice. She's a siren if there ever was one. Only a dead man could have kept his eyes closed. Boomie got Lazarus to blink his eyes and look up at her. Perhaps he even fell in love with her way back then. Who knows? Perhaps she fell in love with him. In any case, he awakened. Then she stepped back, and it was my turn.

I showed him my funny face. I turned down my mouth and twisted my nose and wiggled my ears and waggled my eyebrows, I puffed up my cheeks and jiggled my chin and stuck out my tongue . . . and, by golly, all those years of making kids laugh paid off. From down there in the grave, the child in the frightened man welled up. Despite himself, Lazarus laughed.

Children in the park heard. They slipped off the swings. They dropped from the rings and the bars and slid down the slide, they flew off the carousels and abandoned the teeter-boards and came running to see the gang of clowns raising laughter from the man in the grave. After me, Mamouli took her turn making Lazarus laugh, followed by Polyphemus and Bimba and Bimbo and, last of all, making his eyes sparkle like jewels down in a mine, Papouli did his uproarious Santa Claus face looking down the chimney. The children clamored to have their faces painted so they could look down too, but we told them they had to go home and bring back a dollar and pay it to the attendant dozing in his booth before we'd let them use our make-up. So they did, bringing their parents back with them. When the adults heard that uncannily happy laughter down at the bottom of the shaft, they got up the nerve to join us. Parents and children in funny faces lined up to make Lazarus laugh even louder.

By the end of the day, there was a line of clowns all around the park. And when we ran out of make-up, people found they could look just as funny without it. So we said goodbye to Lazarus, knowing that he would be raised up soon. We didn't expect to see him again; we just told him how nice it was to have met him at last and we journeyed on.

Lazarus did come up out of the ground, the very next day, and there's a new hospital in that town, called the Lazarus Memorial, to prove it. But he never let himself be buried again. His experience had given him a longing to get out of the earth and into the air. (You can understand now why he feels such a kinship to Mamouli.) And he remembered Boomie's voice and her radiant white face. So Boomie didn't just chance upon him, you see. He had been searching for us and knew our caravan was due to pass on that road that day. His face had been shrouded when he lay in the grave, and Boomie was the only one to recognize him; and, of course, the rest of us wore painted faces, so he didn't know which of us was which. But he already loved us before we loved him. In his heart, he was already part of our family. Such are miracles. Thus does God laugh and play and have his little jokes. And how was I to know that I would be the one to start the laughter that still lingers under his sad mouth?

15 🖋

THE SOLOMONS almost killed Lazarus this morning while he was practicing his whitefaced-clown routine. Dad leaped in and pulled them off just in the nick of time. The lad is certainly taking his knocks.

After you've been in the circus a number of years, you come to assume that certain truths are universally known — like the fact that chimps will never appear in the same ring with a clown unless the clown has gone to the trouble of convincing them he's human. Sadmouth clowns who only smile when they're hurt are particularly vulnerable to the fury of the apes. The famous Emmet Kelly was said to be terrified of chimps and would never perform until he had personally made peace with each chimp on the premises.

Chimps, you see, tend to mistake clowns for weakling degenerates of their own species. They are natural Darwinians when it comes to survival of the fittest. And when they see what they take to be a sick chimp out there clowning around, their instinct is to kill him on the spot in order to maintain the purity of the race.

A sad clown is a particular threat, since his sadness clearly indicates that he has tried to make sense out of life. His nonsense shows him to be an ape, but his attempt to make sense proves he's a corrupt one.

The Scandinavian clown, Minnesota Mouth, made the mistake back in 1936 of guest performing in a German circus where the chimps had not been checked out or chained. He was doing a backflip pratfall off a banana peel while reading *Mein Kampf* when three chimps rushed him so fast he was knocked senseless before he ever hit the ground. The leader of the tribe bit that downturned Minnesota mouth right off and gobbled it up with a grin. Such stories of chimp attacks are rife among comics and clowns.

I am not being strictly accurate when I refer to the innate Darwinism of chimps, for they in no wise believe in evolution. In fact, they eschew belief altogether. They are, if anything, hysterical devolutionists eager to get back to the primal Chaos, never to venture into the clear light of the Cosmos again.

Polyphemus says that chimps carry in their huge prefrontal lobes a strong misplaced memory of Eden. I do not wish to offend the fundamentalist, but in truth I must put it down here that if the collective memory of chimps is to be trusted, Adam and Eve left paradise long before they lost their chatter. It was the apes' attempt to make sense out of chatter that turned their bodies bald, uncozying them from that furry state which all meditating beings have been attempting to cuddle back up to ever since.

I wish Polyphemus could take my pen in hand and expound the ape theology. All I know is that the inhabitants of the Garden lived in a state of pure nonsense. The senses were extremely alert, but nobody tried to use the brain to make anything of them. God spoke, like everyone else, in gibberish (sounds whose meaning is purely in their resonance), and, while His promptings were followed without fail, nobody tried to analyze what He said, let alone believe in divine existence or attribute gender to Him.

Chimps in our day are playing a waiting game. They know only too well that the future rests with humankind. Ironically, hope springs up in them precisely where we feel hopeless — namely, in the increased nonsensicality of human behavior. I think we have begun to raise their expectations that we will devolve into them.

But I was telling about the attack on Lazarus. Dare I digress still further? Why not, Bob? You just want to tell about the time you took the Solomons to Yankee Stadium. No! You must stick to the point.

I'll only say this by way of a caution: Never take chimps to a baseball game. The chatter from the dugout and the outfield drives them into homicidal rages. If you want to please them, take them to see an old-fashioned rock concert. Chimps love to watch a public tantrum, provided that it gives no suggestion of intelligence at work. If they get carried away by the joy of chaos, however, the only way I know to silence them — and it's cruel — is to take them to the zoo. Five minutes in the zoo will hush them for a week. One last warning: Don't take a chimp for a walk on Sunday until well past the time the churches let out.

Where was I?

The attack on Lazarus:

We had assembled in the Ring of the Sun for our usual chaotic meditation before breakfast. Our teachers are Mr. and Mrs. Solomon. Chimps are past masters of the art. I say "past masters" because their education in sign language, action painting and the like is gradually diminishing their powers.

The capacity to speak inspired gibberish and create pure chaos are simian talents that every circus performer must acquire, especially the clowns. One cannot make sense without first making nonsense. According to Papouli — who got it from Bimbo and Bimba — it is essential for humans to live in a balanced relationship with apes, because humans have too much of the former and apes have too much of the latter. There is the angry nonsense of the baboon and the gentle, laconic nonsense of the gorilla (Dad forgives humans their weaknesses and even likes to indulge them). But the pure nonsense of the chimpanzees seems most effective.

Much is already known about gibberish, thanks to the glossolaliasts, political evangelists, news broadcasters, sufis, sales pitchmen, barkers and standup comedians. I myself have earned the Solomon Black Belt in Body Gibberish and hope, if I ever rise to the next chakra, to earn one in the style of voice gibberish called *scat*.

The aim of our circus, of course, is to imitate the Cosmos, to suggest the harmony of the spheres, the balanced intelligence of perfect order symbolized in the illusion of the body's flight through the heavens. (Didn't think I had that down, did you, Papouli?) The ideal we hope to inspire, though it would be spiritual conceit actually to possess it (says our chief), is to walk on air. That is what Boomie's boomerangs and birds, Mamouli's flight from the cannon, the leap of the dolphins, the twins on the trampoline and trapeze, the flight of Pegasus, Annie's huge lightness of foot, the leaps of the poodles and dolphins through the hoop, the dance on the wire and the juggling on high all mean to suggest.

But all these acts must be preceded by the destruction of order. That's where apes and clowns and wrestlers in the muck come in. We create the Chaos out of which the Cosmos is reordered, and chimps are nature's most chaotic meditators. Every morning they help us break down what we must build up again; and in the evening they do the same for the audience. Their bicycling and roller-skating is the tame stuff they fake just so they can really fling those bikes around, kick off their skates, rip off their clothes, scramble up poles, bare their fangs, hang upside down, fling their arms about and otherwise throw tantrums. Every morning we humans talk gibberish and throw tantrums too. Then we're ready for the stillness and silence that precede disciplined practice.

How could I have forgotten to tell Lazarus he shouldn't come to morning chaos with his face already painted? When the chimps saw that expression of wide-eyed confusion he'd painted above and below his eyes and around his mouth, they took him for a chimp sickened by thought. Poor lad. It smarts to think about it. The Solomons may be getting on in years, but their teeth are still vicious.

They've made their peace with him now. They know he's nowhere close to an ape. As soon as Mamouli had sewn up his chin, I took Lazarus right over to the Solomons' wagon. Dad held them while Lazarus stripped down and let them sniff his this and that. Then we played a round of bridge, looked at the newspapers, watched TV, passed the bottle and the cigarettes and shared a few noddings and shakings of the head about the state of the world. Once they saw by his expression that Lazarus understood what he was reading and watching and playing, understood what he was worrying about and what he was doing to himself when he smoked and drank, they knew he was just another anxious human being. They'll leave him alone now and learn to love him, I'm quite confident.

Something interesting: Even on TV they're asking themselves the same question we are. They were showing an old movie of the Ali-Spinks heavyweight championship fight. Before the fight, they interviewed Spinks's manager, and I copied down what he said. Lazarus read it over and over again with increasing excitement. I think the glaze of human ambition in his eyes firmly convinced the Solomons that Lazarus was not their kind.

"Ali looks awful and Leon should whip him," the manager said. "Except one thing keeps eating at me. Ali's got some mystical thing about him, a guardian angel or something. That scares the hell out of me. How can you prepare for the mystical?"

"How indeed?" Lazarus, with his injured jaw, kept muttering. "How indeed?"

16 ✎

MAMOULI CAME TO ME this morning to talk over a problem. She has a big one. Great! I love it when people bring me huge, whopping problems I can really mull over. I should have been a psychoanalyst or a priest. If I were a priest, I'd spend my time in that neat little confession box with my ear right up to the grill, imbibing the lamentations, the muttered self-deprecations, the father-forgive-me's. I'd be so grateful for their confessions, I wouldn't make them so much as say a Hail Mary. I'd just say, "Thank you, my child; now run along and send me some of your friends."

I can't help myself. I just don't feel comfortable with people who don't want to share their emotional difficulties with me. People know this, and I often think they come to me to unload, just to make me feel good. I don't deny that I need to hear what's troubling them worse than they need to tell it. But in this regard I'm no different from any of the people I know in the psychology professions. I myself once joined a group-therapy session, just to help a psychiatrist we all rather pitied gain a greater sense of his own worth.

Polyphemus is the only one in our circus who pretends he has no need to unload. Psychic pride, I call it. How can you warm up to a person with no problems to share? Polyphemus belongs back in the freak show. I'm sorry. I take that back. My weakness, not his. But tell me, doesn't having somebody's problem to carry about as your confidential secret make you feel a little bit more like you belong?

To be in the know. To have something to worry about. That's the stuff of life. Something right in your own ken. I feel sorry for people who have to harvest their problems secondhand from the media. Me, I prefer a direct problem fresh from the source, something I wouldn't gossip about (I'm not that sort, despite what you may think), but something I can put in my notebook for people to get nice and anxious about later, just for the fun of it, when it won't do any harm.

Papouli says this is a female trait of mine, but I say he's a chauvinist for saying so, and that's *his* problem; and he'll probably be over to talk about it sooner or later, because, make fun of me as he may for having such a ready ear, he's been over to see me plenty. I know things about you, Papouli, that you don't even know you've told me. Who else knows that you still feel like a virgin because you never slept with anyone but Mamouli, and that you used to brag to her in the old days about all the pretty ladies you'd slept with, because you were embarrassed to have her think you loved her so much and were so pure. You still wonder — shall I tell this? — what a woman looks like down there and what she feels like, as if Mamouli weren't a woman at all. After the twins started getting too much attention, you began to compete by becoming the oldest and most pampered child. You dream of making love with Boomie and then coming home and telling Mamouli all about it and having her take your head on her breast and weep and forgive you. I know all this. I know you envy Lazarus. You get cramps sometimes coaching Boomie, you want her so badly. Your balls feel like they're going to explode. You pretend Mamouli is Boomie (perhaps your greatest circus feat) when you make love. Then, to relieve yourself even more, you sneak over to talk to me after she's asleep.

I write in this notebook sometimes just to make sure I won't blurt out what I know. Writing is a sublimation. With your fear of social humiliation, I'm sure you'd kill me if I disgraced you. Mamouli says you've never felt the same about her since she disgraced you that night she wiggled on her belly in public. Yes, she broke down last night and confessed it and I quoted to her from the *Tao:* "Welcome disgrace as a pleasant surprise." She knew she wasn't walking on air. She thought so at first, but at the end, when she saw that people in the crowd weren't gazing up in amazement, she knew it was all a horrible self-deception. Not that you'll ever know she knew — at least not until you retire. Meanwhile, it's my secret and it sure feels good to have it in my bag, I must admit.

The fact is, Papouli, that I'm like the common lot of humanity. I love your weaknesses more than I love your strength, though it's your strength I ultimately rely on. I find it touching that you always have to hurry over the morning after a night you snuck over, when Mamouli was asleep, to relieve yourself with a long talk. You always have to hurry on over to tell me you made the whole thing up, just to show you weren't only my boss but my friend as well. You can never tell me your problems without making fun of me later for listening to them and believing they really exist. That's all right. I understand. Life, as you say, is not a problem to be solved but a joy to be lived. I agree. We should discourage people when they come to us to whine or complain or seek our sympathy. We should insist that they either come to us in a positive, creative spirit or else stay in their solitary space until they've worked their problems out by themselves. When a person comes to the circus he leaves his problems behind, and we, the performers, should set the example. I agree, I agree, and damn it, Bob, the next time somebody comes to moan and groan you're going to say, cut it out, I've had enough of all that, I want you to tell me your visions, give me your gift.

But I'm glad I indulged myself one last time, Papouli, because I would feel very left out if I didn't know that you, who mock your wife's yearning to defy gravity, are as weighed down as she is. I must say, as a confirmed bachelor, that I had never understood the enormous problem created when two people do not tuck up against each other properly while they're in bed asleep. I had assumed that tucking up was merely a way to keep warm or express affection. I'm glad that Mamouli enlightened me on the subject and that I was able to suggest the way out of this difficulty.

• •

If I were to write a marriage manual . . . fat chance: I, who have had a thousand women and never been with one. But if I were to write a marriage manual, clinger that I am, I would stress not so much the importance of proper sex as of proper holding. I would stress the unspoken rule of balance in the ritual of belly-to-back, or what some couples call "making spoons."

I learned this from Mamouli:

During the course of the night it is extremely important that each partner spend as much time holding as being held. We have no right to sit in the lap of our beloved when we lie on our side in sleep, with his or her arm thrown over us and his or her face pressed to our back, unless we are willing to reverse the position at regular intervals, unless this instinct has ingrained itself so deeply into our nocturnal sense of marital justice that we make the turns without even waking up.

The reason one partner holds the other tucked into his or her body, you see, is so that the other can travel into the astral realm while being held safely to the ground. Until recently, Mamouli had her night flights just as Papouli had his. Their laps were, for each other, like seats in a space vehicle. They were each other's launching pads. Now, even this has been taken from Mamouli.

Papouli climbs into bed each night and, facing the wall, reaches back, pulls Mamouli hard against him, installs his rear firmly in her lap, tugs her arm over and clamps it securely under his, against his chest, then drops off to sleep and is up and away in no time. He doesn't return until morning. Mamouli no longer gets her turn. Astral greed has possessed him.

Or is it a deliberate refusal to let her leave the ground

even in sleep? He tells her he's afraid she won't be able to handle herself out there any more; she's become too astrally giddy. But doesn't he, as king and master of the circus, fear that she might genuinely be able to walk on air and that her astral journey will help her gain the experience necessary for showing it to the world?

I don't mind sleeping alone, because I don't like to leave anything behind, least of all my body — not even for a few hours in the night. I used to trip out into the infinite spaces of night flight, but the slightest noise made me fall horribly from heights unspeakable, saved from crashing only because I was suddenly jolted awake before I hit the ground. Now, just to be safe, I sleep in a bed of soft poodles. I leave all that spiritual sightseeing to the more adventurous. I lack what you might call the Chinese perspective. I'd rather look up at a landscape than down. All the same, I maintain that it's a crime when, in bed at night, one partner hogs the astral while the other, holding tight so the loved one won't slip away forever, doesn't even receive the reward of a trip of her own.

I wonder if I gave Mamouli the right advice. Refuse to get under the covers with him again unless he agrees to tuck himself up against your back the way he used to and lets you ride out into space on just as many journeys as he takes. If he gives you a hard time, tell him you'll sleep with Annie in the straw. *She'll* send you on a trip.

17 🌀

Everyone's teaching Lazarus how to fall. That's something we circus folk understand in depth (ho ho). You can't learn how to keep your balance until you've learned how to lose it.

Lazarus can fall from a ball, he can fall from a wall, from a horse and a rope and a wire. Gradually his act raises him higher and higher. He's slung when he falls, thrown and blown and twirled when he falls. He's the falling fool who falls on his head, on his tail, on his shoulder and knee and elbow and face, until every part of him carries the ache of his ambition. And, oh, does Mamouli love to play the healer! She's rubbed more herbs into his body than I knew existed out there in the meadowlands. When Annie the Elephant and Mamouli go for their walks in the country, they now spend all their time looking for the mineral muds they bring home in big bags to smear over him from head to foot. The other day I found him in front of the Papouli wagon, covered thick with dry mud. He was hardened like a statue, with his arms spread out, healing in the heat with only a few holes for his eyes, mouth and nose, until Mamouli came out with a sledgehammer and busted him open. He said he felt wonderful, good as new again, ready for the night's performance.

So here's Lazarus in his parody of a tumbler's costume. The moment the crowd sees him, laughter breaks out. Children jump up, pointing. Full of confidence, he strides up the track, trips over a pile of horseshit, does a flip and sprawls out on his chest, but not without spreading his arms like a bird in flight, as if it were all part of his act and he did it on purpose, though you can see the front of his leotard is ripped and he's bleeding. And, look, he climbs to the top of our ape-human pyramid. He stands on one foot with a triumphant grin, then totters wildly and crashes to the sawdust. See Lazarus interrupt the elephant act to be lifted at the waist in Annie's trunk and flung, at the moment of his greatest posturing, into the dolphin tank. See him fly out of the water, tossed high by Jack and Jill into the arms of the gorilla, then spun, flung and bam! he hits the wall of the tent. Or here's Lazarus asking Mamouli if he can have a turn being shot from the cannon. He shinnies up the barrel, pokes his head in to see what it's like in there and, oops, he's slipped inside. Here comes Mamouli with a brand of fire. She lights the fuse. But does Lazarus zoom out as she did, across the arena into the net? No, he dribbles limply from the cannon's nose, flops backward onto the seat of Boomie's motorcycle, which lunges forth, leaps over three barrels before it flings the rider off and sends him rolling across the ground to whack against a pole so hard he wraps around it, and I have to pry him off with a pitchfork while the whole tent shakes with laughter.

Lazarus has only twelve more feet to go before he can fall from the highwire. Then he'll be ready for the Greatest Fall on Earth. The only part he has to correct is when he gets up looking sad after a fall. Papouli says he's not ever to wipe his eyes with his fist the way I do when I'm playing my bum on his bum having a bummer. Lazarus should increase the sadness on his mouth before he falls, but he should always come up smiling. The greater the fall, the greater the smile. His mouth should grow sad only as the pain subsides and the confidence returns. The audience has to get used to the idea that Lazarus will smile no matter what happens to him, as if every accident terrifies him out of the horrors of unhappiness into smiling again for dear life.

"When you finally fail to come up smiling," Papouli told Lazarus, "you'll break their hearts. Then you'll do what neither the king's horses nor the king's men could do. Polyphemus calls it the Humpty-Dumpty plan. You'll put their hearts back together again, and yours will be mended as well. The smile that breaks out on your face after you've died and been born again is going to fill us all with such great joy, my boy, that every person in the tent will become one in the power of comic resurrection. The last laugh is going to belong to you. You're going to enter the pantheon of the seventh heaven. I'm going to send you up to the place where the Great Grand-Papouli once floated, and the grounding current of a woman's love is going to bring you back down again!"

We were seated at the banquet table outdoors when he

116

told us this, and Mamouli, almost by reflex, stood up beaming. *"I'm* going to bring him down?"

"Not this time, sweetheart. Boomie is. Aren't you, darling?"

Then it was Boomie who beamed. She rested her head on her lover's shoulder. Mamouli's mouth fell as she sat down slowly. She gazed off toward the hills. Poor Mamouli. She hates to be left out where love's concerned.

18 ✥

If my handwriting is hard to read, that's because my hand is shaking. It's shaking because I've been sitting here in my wagon through the early hours, with my fists clenched so tight there are cuts on my palms from the press of my fingernails. I would like so badly to punch that son of a bitch, Papouli, right in his big, pompous gut. I know we have to show some kind of respect for our leader, or the whole family will collapse. But let me tell you, Papouli, if you want to regain my respect you're going to have to do some heavy apologizing to Mamouli, and if I ever hear you talk that way about her again, I swear to God I'm going to beat the shit out of you, I don't care how big you are.

• •

Such are the crisscrossings of our lives that the event Papouli spoke to Lazarus about with such cruelty and indiscretion was caused indirectly by the fact that Lazarus was playing in the same town we were, that night some two years ago. For that matter, you could say I was at fault. I had fallen into the bad habit of scheduling our arrival for shortly after the departure of Lazarus.

But we got there too early this time. It was a poor town, and the people were trying to raise nothing less than a cathedral with Lazarus's burial. He had been down for a week, and the money wasn't quite paid up yet. When our circus parade passed along Main Street, we could hear the voice of the mayor or the bishop — someone important — urging people to dig deep in their pockets and put out one more large bill for another look at Lazarus. Then a girl's voice pleaded with the people not to let the dear, good man lie down there any longer, to show their love and compassion before he froze or starved to death and the town had to live forever in shame for its hardness of heart.

We heard all this as we rode past locked stores and empty sidewalks on a Sunday afternoon, and we knew that we wouldn't have our usual sellout audience that night. We were heading back to camp along the road that led to the city dump, Mr. Solomon in the lead on his roller skates, with his wife right behind him on the bicycle; the four Papoulis on Annie's back; Pegasus clopping along beside them, with me in the saddle and Fetch on the rump, and Boomie on her flying motorcycle bringing up the rear.

Mamouli started to nag Papouli again, saying that this would be an ideal time for her to try to walk on air. To our surprise, Papouli agreed, provided she start not from the high platform, the way she always wanted to, but more modestly this first time, from a platform on the ground. If she could walk up into the air to join him and the twins on the wire, he said, then as far as he was concerned she could do whatever she pleased from then on and he'd back her all the way. Meanwhile, he hoped she wouldn't mind if he and the twins tried out the new propeller helmet they'd invented. "Of course not. That's perfect," Mamouli said, and everybody was excited, though it was clear that Papouli was just trying literally to get Mamouli off his back for a night. He wanted to try the highwire walk without her. The twins had fashioned a steel helmet with a knob at the top, to which a bar flatter than his usual balancing bar could be attached as a kind of propeller. With this on his head, Papouli had been practicing a vibration of his neck that made the propeller whirl faster and faster. He hoped that with the twins whirling as littler propellers at either end of the large one, he could be momentarily lifted off the wire. But obviously there was no way Mamouli could continue to sit on his shoulders juggling. So he figured that with such a small crowd expected he and the twins could try their experiment and Mamouli could try hers, with no harm done.

He and Mamouli argued all the rest of the way as to whether Papouli should take his disbelief out of the tent while she performed, since she would need the absolute faith of everyone present. But Papouli insisted that he knew how to suspend his disbelief, and the whole point was for her to join her family on the wire. Faith was a trick like any other, he said, and he was enough of a pro to have mastered it. "You just don't look earthward," he said.

Seeing that he wasn't going to yield, Mamouli finally

convinced herself that he would be able to muster faith in her. She became almost hysterically excited. I built her a nifty little platform in the Ring of the Sun. Bimbo painted astrological signs all around the edge, and a launching spot at the center. Bimba chanted magical incantations. Boomie wheeled into town, filled a bottle with holy water from the font of the Catholic church, said a prayer to the image of Our Lady of Heaven, and hurried back to sprinkle the water on the place where Mamouli would stand. We helped Mamouli put together a special costume with a long white silk gown, a sky-blue satin robe, Boomie's necklace of silver crescent moons, and golden slippers. Papouli, to show his good faith, wove a floral wreath. Mamouli looked radiant.

There were only fifty or sixty spectators, it's true, but they seemed ready to cooperate. I asked them please not to stay so scattered out, to crowd in close so that we could draw on their combined energy for what was to follow, and they eagerly did so. Then I imitated the blast of a trumpet, and Papouli, with the twins, began the new propeller act. The contraption wobbled somewhat, but it worked pretty well. After that was over, the twins dropped the propeller to me and slid down the ropes, leaving Papouli up there balanced on the wire just above the platform where Mamouli was to perform. She entered the circle with dynamic confidence, and we all cheered lustily, to get the crowd going. Papouli reached above his head for the top mike and lowered it to where she stood. Our audience sensed the importance of what was to follow. A hush fell over us all. I looked up and saw that Papouli was wafting gracefully on the wire with arms outspread, not looking down, but straight ahead in what appeared to be utmost concentration. I joined the others in fixing my eyes on Mamouli, as she began to speak in a strangely timid, tight voice, like a little girl. She said that she was going to perform an act she had been preparing since she was small, an act which expressed her faith that some urge to higher consciousness sleeps in each of us. When aroused, she said, it can lift us from the ground and carry our bodies wherever we wish to journey.

"My dear ones," she said, her voice stronger now, more husky and maternal. "I could never walk on air, as I did when I was a child and am about to do again, without your uplifting presences. I have learned to love all of you out there and to rely on you. I offer you this miracle as my humble gift. Please accept it."

I made the sound of a rolling drum, then pressed a button that reeled the microphone up to the top of the tent.

Mamouli brought her feet together in a circle of blue at the center of the platform. She crouched down, pressed her arms against her body. The cords in her neck tightened. She clenched her teeth, spread her fingers —

You can guess the rest when I tell you that Papouli cleared his throat just then.

From up there on the wire came the sound of phlegm being hawked up. It was more than cruel, and I have tried to forget it. I have always admired Mamouli for trying to overcome it, even though a spell, once broken, is impossible to restore. Eyes blinked in the crowd, and I myself lost my attention for an instant. It seemed that everyone was clearing his throat at once, before silence resumed.

Yes, you can guess the rest, and I would as soon forget that night. Papouli put the propeller hat away. He never tried that act again with the twins. But to my absolute disgust, he has been the only one of us who has the bad taste to refer to that night when he wants to throw a particularly cruel jibe at Mamouli, as if he were simply blind to the fact that her failure was his own stupid fault. Who taught us about never breaking concentration? And who's always screaming that interruption is the greatest sin of the twentieth century?

• •

The way Papouli brought up the night I have just described was more than cruel. It was devastating.

The theme was set by Lazarus, whom I found lying on the floor of the dressing room after our performance yesterday evening, panting, exhausted, his white leotard torn and smeared with blood. I carried him to the Papouli wagon, and Mamouli got right to work bringing him back. She stripped him down this time and unwrapped her acupuncture needles, so I stuck around for a visit. (I love to watch the way she vibrates those needles. Sometimes she just puts the needles in, sits back and sings until they begin to gyrate. You can actually hear them humming in the flesh.)

Dad and Papouli stomped up the steps, barged in noisily and threw themselves on the bed, Dad sucking on his whiskey bottle while Papouli, euphoric, rapped away about Lazarus, praising his performance to the skies, without the least sensitivity to the fact that he was interrupting a healing.

"If you think that was a belly flop you did tonight," he

said to the lad, "you should have seen Mamouli the night she walked on air." He guffawed and Dad, trying hard not to laugh too, blew whiskey in a spray all over the room.

Mamouli told Papouli to cut it out, but in a nice voice, keeping her good humor out of concern for Lazarus.

Papouli whacked her playfully on the behind. "JoJo, the dogfaced lady," he croaked. "She walks, she talks, she karrrawls on her belly like reptile. She's almost human!"

"Has Dad been sharing that bottle with you?" she said. She pulled the needles out of Lazarus and started on him with her thumbs. Papouli sat up and looked at Lazarus, who lay with his head turned sideways, smiling in utmost contentment.

"I can't remember when's the last time Mamouli gave *me* a massage like that," Papouli said.

Lazarus sat right up on the table, blushing. He hopped to the floor and, with a grandiose gesture, signaled for Papouli to lie down on the table. "Your turn," he said. "Right, Mamouli?"

But Papouli pushed Lazarus back to the table. "I was only kidding, kid. Lie down. Enjoy. You were so terrific out there tonight! You'll be at the top soon!" He pointed upward and proclaimed with a forced expression, "Our star! Successor to the Great Grand-Papouli!"

Lazarus lay back on the table hesitantly, on his stomach, as Mamouli began to pound his back with the edges of her hands. "Doesn't that feel good," Papouli said. He threw an arm over Dad's shoulder, and the two of them whispered together for a time, like a couple of schoolboys. Then Papouli stood, spread his arms and began to sweep up and down the wagon on ballet toes, telling the story with mincing, poetic mockery as Dad, seated on the sideboard, puffed fast on his cigar.

Papouli told how the eyes of the crowd were fixed on Mamouli like beams of energy, lifting her ever higher. She soared off the platform, he said, whirled and danced on air. "Didn't you, sweetheart?"

He stopped his dance to look down at Lazarus. He winked. "Up toward the wire she rose. Her body spread out flat now, she swam through the air. She didn't want to surprise me yet, she wasn't ready to stand beside me, you see, while I still relied, poor earthbound me, on the wire under my feet. First she had to fly around the entire arena, rolling and swooping over the heads of the amazed visionaries. Why, she might have slipped through the hole at the top of the tent and swum out amongst the cosmic whales, had not her curiosity about the crowd's reaction got the better of her. Isn't that right, sweetheart?"

"Cut it out," I said.

"She wanted to see their amazement. Vanity o'erwhelmed her. She looked down." Papouli nudged Lazarus. "What do you think she saw?"

Lazarus hid his face in his arms and shrugged.

"Did she see faces gazing up in rapture? I'm afraid not, my boy. What she saw were people with their heads lowered, embarrassed spectators muttering to one another, wishing they hadn't come, biting their lips or looking toward the exit as if they just couldn't wait to escape our tent."

Through all this, I watched Mamouli from the corner where I stood in the Papouli wagon. She was not allow-ing the tears to well up this time. Papouli hoisted himself beside Dad, took the cigar from the gorilla's mouth, puffed on it a few times and put it back.

"Then did our poor Mamouli realize she wasn't up in the air at all. She was down on the stage on her belly, wriggling and squirming and thrashing about, her face uplifted in idiot joy!"

Lazarus pushed up from the table and was out of the wagon without a word before his feet had hardly touched the ground. Mamouli's face was grotesque with pain now. My fists clenched. I fought hard to keep myself from smashing Papouli right in the kisser before he could say another word. But I didn't. I have this belief — Never mind. I'm a coward. I stood there.

Mamouli looked at him for a moment with eyes ablaze. "You tell this in front of him!" she screamed. "You've robbed me of his faith! Thief!"

"Call me what you like!" Papouli screamed back. "He had to hear. You've sold him on helping you try it again, goddam it! I know you have! I can't let you do that!"

Mamouli stepped up to him and hit him hard across one cheek with her right hand, then across the other with her left hand. He didn't so much as flinch. He grabbed her by the shoulders and pulled her against him while she struggled. "I love you, woman!"

She broke away. He grabbed her again and shook her. "I can't let you kill yourself. You're subject to mortal laws. Can't you get that through your dreamy head? You'll crash-land next time! With a big, fat splat!"

That's when I went to hit him. And I think ·I would have. But Dad was on me just like that. He picked me up and carried me outside. I figured he was going to bash my brains out or something, not that I cared at that point. But it's strange. Instead, he lugged me to my wagon, lay me down, gazed tenderly upon me for a time, blinked his coal-like eyes and patted me gently on the cheek. He bent over and whispered something with whiskey breath, and — did I imagine this? — he kissed me with his big rubber lips, flicked out the light and quietly left me.

He made me feel so good that it took hours of lying there before my fists began to clench and the rage rose in me once more. But with this entry, I've released it. I'm ready for a good, long sleep.

19 🖋

I AM TAKING THIS OCCASION to retract any violent fantasies I may have had toward Papouli. I am pulling my punch, so to speak. In this circus, hitting someone in the gut is an expression of fun and affection, and I don't want to spoil that tradition. If I ever throw a punch into Papouli's gut, I promise not to do so until he gives me the Houdini wink, which Papouli says the Great Great Grand-Papouli, an aerial magician, learned directly from the famous illusionist. Houdini, as you may remember, was killed by a punch in the gut when the wink didn't take.

The Houdini wink is reserved for adult male bully types. It is a form of hypnotism that I would be happy to demonstrate to all my readers, however, male or female. Don't worry, I won't put you very deeply under. You'll have no trouble coming out of it, and you won't make a fool of yourself.

So: If you're interested in being hypnotized, please

hold this book directly in front of your face. Okay? Now. Put your knees together and breathe deeply, making your stomach go out as you breathe the air in, and in as you breathe the air out. Good. That's known as deep breathing, and, actually, you should breathe that way all the time. Close your eyes and open them again three times, squeezing your eyelids firmly together. Fine. This is going very well. I hope you stay with me. Nothing unpleasant is going to happen to you. Quite the opposite. You'll actually want to do this kind of hypnotism for your friends, so let's relax our neck and shoulders. Relax the whole body, breathing nice and easy. Clear your throat. Meow softly like a cat. Pant like a happy dog. That's good. Now . . .

Wake up! If you did everything I asked you to in the last paragraph, you were hypnotized. That's all there is to it. Hypnotism is just a willingness to go along. And that's the way it is with the Houdini wink.

Sometimes Papouli hangs around after the show to talk to the children. Little girls always seem to express their affection to him the way they do to little boys, by kicking him. Papouli loves to be kicked by little girls. Little boys like to hit him. He loves that too. He sticks his stomach out and says to some tough boy, "Throw a punch into that." The kid lays back, puffs up his cheeks and bams one in for all he's worth. Tough boys adore Papouli for letting them do that to none other than the celebrated ringmaster and star performer of the circus. But now and then some bully father gets a leer in his eye and wants to have a shot at Papouli's belly too. "You wouldn't mind if I tried a punch?" one of these oafs will ask, as he sways from side to side bulging his shoulder muscles. Papouli shrugs. "Go right ahead," he says, taking a firm stance and presenting the full, hard roundness of his belly.

Then the showoff father doubles up his fist and presses his lips hard together and rears back, looking at Papouli one last time to make sure he has permission. That's when Papouli gives him the Houdini wink. This wink tells the father something like this: You're part of The Great Papouli Circus now. Welcome aboard. When you hit me, don't actually do it with all your might. Pull the punch and I'll pretend you doubled me over.

That's the trick, you see. Not knowing how to take a truly violent punch, but just knowing how to give a little wink. Of course, when the kind of man who wants to show he can topple the Great Papouli does pull his punch, Papouli gives him his pride's worth. He lets out a great "Oof!", his eyes bug out, he grabs his stomach, bends over double, staggers about, drops to his knees and groans with pain. Then he clears his head with a shake, looks up with amazement at the man who hit him, puts his hands back with the palms up in a sign of surrender, then reaches out to the man, who proudly pulls Papouli to his feet; and the children jump about, clamoring after their mighty father. Such is circus life.

So, no more talk of punching Papouli unless he first gives me the Houdini wink; and (God rest Harry Houdini) may the wink always work!

20 ✍

THERE ARE DAYS like today when I'm grateful I have
the job of shoveling dung. I wouldn't want to be just sitting around thinking about what happened this morning, after meditation, when Papouli unveiled the details
of the Humpty-Dumpty plan. "Too dangerous!" wailed
Mamouli. "You want to get him killed!" She threw her
arms around Lazarus and hugged him fervently. He
struggled to break free.

"Who doesn't have faith now?" asked Papouli.
"Lazarus isn't worried. Are you, son?"

Lazarus extricated himself from Mamouli and went to
stand calmly beside our chief. "I'll be fine," he said.

This just made Mamouli clutch her hands at her breast
and implore the heavens. She followed us out of the tent,
weeping loudly. "You have no right!" she kept shouting,
until Boomie started to cry too, though she stopped
when Mamouli screamed out that Boomie's love hadn't

been tested yet. "We don't even know whether it can be *called* love. It could be just another infatuation."

This really got Boomie's dander up. She dried her tears fast and threw such a look at Mamouli that I was glad she didn't have her boomerangs on hand. Boomie proudly gave her stump arm to Lazarus and marched him off to her wagon.

"Well, you said you loved the Comb! You said you loved He-Power!" Mamouli screamed after them. Boomie made a vulgar sign without turning to answer. That was the first unbeautiful thing I think I've ever seen Boomie do. Even her acts of violence were never vulgar.

I don't know where I stand on all this. We *are* taking a huge chance with the lad. But isn't that the way he wants it? Is Mamouli really trying to protect him, or is she just after taking the top position for herself? I don't know. I'll get back to work. Dung shoveling is such a comfort.

• •

At the edge of the corral, there's a beetle trying to push a ball of dung up over a muddy ridge made by the rut of a tire. Now and then I put aside my shovel, sit on the fence and watch him. Then I write in this notebook. Writing and shoveling have a lot in common. They're both ways to clean up.

The patience of this dung beetle amazes me. He's been trying to get that ball up the hill all morning. Every time he has it almost to the top, he loses control and it rolls back down to the bottom again. I've named him Sisyphus. Here comes Mrs. Sisyphus. See how she climbs right on top of the dung ball. And now here's Papouli, still in his long johns, scratching his belly. He watches while the beetle rolls the ball and Mrs. Sisyphus scrambles to stay balanced on top.

"Just like a woman," he says. "Always taking the free ride." Papouli climbs onto the fence and sits. I think I'll get back to shoveling.

• •

The dung beetles are still at it. Mr. Sisyphus keeps pushing the ball up the hill. The wife rides along, making the ball heavier. When her husband loses control, she falls off and the ball rolls back down for the fiftieth time. The twins have come to watch. I tell them what Papouli said.

"Listen, Pop," says Bimbo. "She's not out for a free ride. She's up there rolling the ball with her feet and keeping it balanced besides. Without her, he'd never get it up and over."

And here's Polyphemus to have his say. "True. The one on top does the balancing, only it's the male. The female is the one pushing the ball."

"So there!" cries Bimba. "Stuff that in your pipe and smoke it, Pop!"

The twins depart in a huff. Papouli slips down from the fence and sits on the ground. Ah! The dung ball's on the crest of the ridge. What a relief to see it roll on toward home. But look, now they're in another valley with an even higher ridge to climb. How I admire the patience of Mr. and Mrs. Sisyphus! If I were ringmaster, I'd give them a spot in the circus. I'm going to shovel up the last of Annie's load.

• •

Oho! They got it up and over. They're side by side now, pushing it across the road nice and easy. Mamouli and Papouli, why can't you get your act together like that? If

Papouli would give the full power of his faith to Mamouli, she'd walk on air, I know she would.

"Papouli. Listen to me," I said just now.

"Listen to you about what?"

"You've said it yourself so many times, when talking about the whole purpose of our circus. 'God help those who have lost their illusions.' Isn't our goal to sustain the illusion?"

"What are you mumbling about, Bobby?" (That's the way he talks to me. I'm not kidding.)

"I'm mumbling about Mamouli. She'd fly. You'd see. She'd fly."

"Why in hell are you worrying about Mamouli at a time like this? She's perfectly all right down here on the ground. It's Lazarus we have to figure out. If you're worried about Mamouli's wailing and gnashing of teeth, be happy. For what Lazarus is going to do, it helps to have a weeping woman or two. It fits into the script."

• •

When everything was cleaned up in the corral, I sat down next to Papouli. We chewed the fat. Lazarus joined us. He said he'd just as soon give up the whole act, if it was going to create a lot of conflict. He said Boomie was starting to get cold feet again.

Papouli patted his knee. "Does she love you, lad?"

Lazarus shrugged.

"Come on, kid, you know she does. If I didn't feel absolutely confident that she was head over heels in love with you, do you think I'd be taking this chance?"

They discussed the situation for quite some time, and I began to suspect, from what Lazarus said, that he and

Boomie were already making plans to flee our circus. There were definite hints of departure.

"Has Boomie told you the story about how Mamouli brought me back from the dead? She hasn't? Ask her to tell it. That'll give her courage. I'd tell you the story myself, but Bob's heard it so many times he's liable to puke if he has to hear it again, and he just got this corral clean. Once Boomie tells you the story of my great fall, you'll understand why I know exactly what I'm doing and why Mamouli knows even better than I do that you're not going to die in this man's circus. You're going to come through in grand style. Go on, now. Ask her to tell you."

So Lazarus went back to Boomie.

I wouldn't have minded telling the story myself. In fact, I'm going to write it down here in my notebook, for posterity. It's the event upon which Polyphemus based his Humpty-Dumpty plan.

21 ✒

THE NIGHT at Barnum-Ringling when the wire broke and Papouli fell with the Great Grand-Papouli under him, Papouli would surely have been killed had he not landed on the body of his father. As it was, he bounced high, drifted down and seemed to settle gently on the sawdust. For a time nothing moved. Then suddenly his body began to fling itself about. He could somehow watch the conflagration inside his own flesh. It was as if there were huge knots of fire in his spine, electric generators discharging upward, sending streaks of voltage crackling from the base of his spine to the top of his head, where they exploded outward with a deafening noise. He couldn't remember how to breathe.

He was aware that the clowns were all around him chattering. The stands seemed to be filled with a horde of titans, as if the gods had suddenly descended to fill the air with their suffocating clamor. The light kept blasting out of his head. He could smell his hair smoking, he could see the silver sparks slither out of the scorched blackness of his bones. His heart began to beat irregularly. He felt it flutter, fold wings, flap once more, desperately, and then WHAM! his heart blew open and blossomed in his chest, while he blasted out of his body, up through a blinding white light to a far corner of the tent, where he found himself looking down without any emotion whatsoever upon the scene below.

There lay his father, next to him. The doctor was taking the old man's pulse. Papouli knew that the Great Grand-Papouli was not in his body either, and he looked around for him. There he was, at the exact level where the wire had been. He was lying flat on his back, eyes closed, smiling.

Papouli looked down at the people in the stands. They were no longer godlike, but dull and somewhat faceless. A crowd was now gathered in the center ring, around the two bodies. He heard someone say, in a doll-like voice, that the father was alive but the son was ice cold and had no pulse. The concern in the voice sounded false, and he could muster no interest in answering the questions put to him.

He even lost interest in his own body and looked again toward the stands with vague curiosity. He saw a young woman in bright apparel rush down an aisle, push an usher aside, climb the rail, run to the circle, shove her way to his body and kneel down beside it. The tone of authority in her voice put her immediately in command.

"John," she said. "Come back. I want you here with me. You belong with me. Come."

Papouli didn't particularly want to go back. A group of

friendly people were somewhere up ahead calling to him to hurry up. He didn't quite recognize them, but they were a cheerful lot, and he was perfectly willing to join them. But the young woman's voice had fastened itself to him. It would not let go.

Her voice was like a solid substance that had bound itself to his heart. Papouli realized that he was loved, and that love is a tangible reality, a path into life. He didn't think this, of course, but he knew it, and he moved right down that shaft of love, back into his body — the greatest tightrope act he would ever perform. His heart, quickened by the urgency of the beautiful voice, resumed its beat. His diaphragm bellowed a rush of air into his lungs. He was carried out, he retched, drank, and was soon well again — ready to ride in the ambulance with his father, seated, holding the old man's hand.

• •

The young woman who saved Papouli, of course, was Mamouli. She had come to love him as she sat in the stands watching him walk the invisible wire. When she visited him in the hospital the next day, bringing flowers for the Great Grand-Papouli, Papouli fell in love with her too. They decided to start a circus of their own, based on the two lessons they had learned the night before. The first lesson was that love is a force that holds us to the earth. It is none other than the call to incarnation. The second was that there are indeed (as the yogis have long claimed) centers of light energy lodged in the spine, charged by breath with the mysterious *prahna*, each radiating spiritual strength into its particular pool of influence; and that when we die they release that energy back into the vaster pools of the universal body, the system of light.

I couldn't hope to imitate Papouli's excitement every time he tells this story. I've tried to tell it as directly as I can, without playing the clown. When Lazarus hears it from Boomie, he'll know exactly what to expect from her if his act is to succeed. She'll have to be for him what Mamouli was for Papouli. Is that possible? If Polyphemus says it is, then it is. I can't remember when he's ever been wrong about anything really important.

22 ✍

LAZARUS HAS INSPIRED US ALL, but especially Mamouli. Even the incomparable Franconi and Ducron, who set the great tradition of equestrian clowns over a hundred years ago, would have raved at what she came up with. I had always found the Mamouli marionette number embarrassing, so much so that I haven't mentioned it before in this book. It was one of those attempts at satire that never quite comes off because the one who pretends to satirize a prejudice is actually enforcing it — like those films that deplore violent sex while awakening our taste for it.

The act was supposed to show how ridiculous a woman appears when she lets herself be manipulated by a man. Papouli thought he was really doing Mamouli a favor when he conceived it. But all I think it suggested was a dumb housewife who was easy to manipulate. The only part I admired was when Dad tied the strings to

Mamouli — no mean feat for an ape close to *delirium tremens*.

Here's how it used to go: I created a diversion in a far corner of the tent by falling in love with a young lady in the audience. A huge rose blossomed from my pocket. I picked it and gave it to her as a proposal of marriage. She turned me down. The rose wilted in my hand. I wept. Meanwhile, Papouli was climbing the wire in the dark. The young lady repented, accepted my proposal, and the rose blossomed again. I offered her my cheek. When she kissed me, more roses blossomed from my buttonholes and a sunflower burst open on my head, while the astonished crowd laughed. The spotlight swept from me and the girl to the track, where Dad was lugging a huge gift box on his back. He set it down in the Sun Ring, untied the ribbon and tore off the wrapping. He turned the box over sideways. Out flopped a limp rag doll dressed in curlers, apron and house slippers. He dragged Mamouli to her feet, stepped back, she collapsed in a heap. After trying this a few more times, he looked up. Papouli appeared on the wire holding his pole. Strings hung down from both ends. Dad tied the strings to Mamouli's hair, hands, knees and feet. Then Papouli, playing the puppet master, brought her to her feet. Pegasus galloped into the ring. The puppet jumped up backward onto the horse's back. Dad threw Mamouli a feather duster, and she began to do an idiot house-cleaning pantomime while Pegasus circled and Papouli pulled the strings.

No, I never found the act satisfying. Granted, a few novice circusgoers may have found it amazing that such a jerky, comic figure as the Mamouli marionette could stay on a horse, but that's such old hat. I can't disclose the exact size of the Sun Ring (it's close to thirteen meters), but everybody who loves circuses already knows that the exact balance of centrifugal and centripetal forces in a perfect ring are such that when you stand on the back of an animal going at a certain speed it's almost impossible to fall off. Papouli certainly had no trouble with the pole. What was there to appreciate, really? And when people can't appreciate, they tend to depreciate. Mamouli knew that and suffered from the mocking tone of the laughter. Besides, we've had a longstanding unspoken agreement that we don't keep any act that gets more laughter from the members of one sex than from the other. The men always laughed much louder . . . Until our last performance, that is, when up scampers Fetch with a pair of sheep shears in his teeth. He leaps onto the horse's rump, the housewife grabs the shears. Before Papouli can figure out what's going on, Mamouli cuts all the strings and returns the shears to Fetch, who leaps off and runs out of the tent, while Mamouli sheds her housewife garb, kicks it away, and look! She's the ethereal Columbine in pink slippers and frilled tutu, no longer floundering about but leaping and whirling on the back of Pegasus with such grace that it seems less that she comes down to touch the horse than that the horse flies up to touch her with his back. The women in the audience respond with a cry — not a shriek or a scream, but a lyrical kind of "Ah!"

Meanwhile, on the wire, Papouli appears to go into a rage. His pole becomes Thor's lightning bolt, and he is about to hurl it down at the liberated woman. But the men support the women now. They roar their disapproval. Papouli yields to their wishes. He lays the pole horizontal in his palms, weighs it with a sad acceptance, then drops it to the floor of the ring. It strikes in such a way that it rises almost perpendicular before it falls to rest; and we can almost see the hands of a clock, as the woman pirouetting on the horse springs high one last time. Pegasus soars to meet her and flies with her out of the tent.

I'll say one thing for Papouli: he went with the changes and improvised beautifully. But he was a maniac afterward, screaming at Mamouli in the dressing room, saying he'd cancel the act if she didn't go back to the old way. He had his rationale, as usual. Get this one: He said we don't espouse the notion, in this circus, that creation comes out of conflict. The act was Mamouli's revenge for an argument he'd been having with her. "I will not have our personal problems taken into the tent and acted out," he said.

Papouli always seems to lose his cool when Mamouli comes up with something new he didn't think of. He'll keep the new act. It's good. It releases tension in the crowd. That's what the first half of the show is supposed to do, and he knows it.

He'll come around.

23 ✐

PAPOULI'S RIGHT. The people love Lazarus much
more, now that he's stopped wiping his eyes with his
fist after he falls, now that he bounces up smiling. When
Lazarus trips over a banana peel and slides across the
gravel of the arena scraping his chin, it's the way he
keeps his smile intact throughout the ordeal that makes
them laugh so insanely. It drives them wild to see him
hit the ground flat on his stomach and bounce up still
grinning from ear to ear. When he cracks his back across
a balancing bar, whirls around, whacks his head on the
ground and staggers about rubbing his head and beaming as if with the greatest pleasure, they go into convul-
sions. I suppose it makes them feel marvelous to think
that someone can even pretend to enjoy such things.
Still, I'm a bit baffled by why people stamp their feet,
grab at their throats, clutch one another as if they were
dying; and all because they've seen someone dominate
his pain. Such laughter is getting to be dangerous.

"Mr. Manager!" I heard someone squeal yesterday. "Come out of that trailer! I want to have a word with you!"

Before I was halfway down the stairs, a hefty fellow in candystriped shirt and suspenders had already started to chew my ear off. He said that at our circus his children all got sick from the laughter and his wife nearly choked to death. She was still in bed with a swollen throat and a ruptured gut, and if she died he was going to sue our circus for plenty.

Polyphemus, hearing the commotion, ambled on over to set the man straight. He said that nobody in history was ever proved to have died from laughing in a circus. The only deaths from laughter are well documented by the Guiness Museum atop the Empire State Building. They occur exclusively among a tribe of headhunters in New Guinea, who eat the human brain. If you consume a brain entirely, Polyphemus said, it's true you giggle yourself to death. But a clown does not even appeal to the brain. He appeals to the idiot parts of the body such as the shoulders, belly and behind.

The man persisted in trying to bully us with his threats. He said a circus that made people sick should be run out of town, no matter what the cause. I think he hoped for a payoff. He told Polyphemus he knew all about giants, too, and had taken precautions, warning the police they had better drive out to our camp and check up on him if he didn't report back in an hour.

"What's this you know about giants?" Polyphemus snarled.

The man shrugged. He started to his car. We followed. He got in, revved up the engine, stuck his head out the window and gave us what passed for a knowing look.

"You folks probably don't believe in the little people. But in our town we do. One of them passed through, and he told us all about what you fellas eat to make yourselves grow so big. You don't get it at no butcher shop either. It's what the medical trade calls *species specificus.* You giants eat the human growth gland. Thought I didn't know that, hunh? You eat the pituitaries. Steal them from the hospitals, or if you can't find them there — "

"Tell your informant he's turned into a boob," Polyphemus said. "To think I hid him in my hat." He shuffled away.

I stood there by the window of the car, watching the blood rise up the man's throat until welts broke out along the creases of his chins. "We had a mass killer in our town back when I was a youngster," he whispered. "Every time they found a body, there was a little cut at the back of the neck. Never did track him down, because each time somebody saw him he was bigger than the time before. Nobody figured he was the same suspect. From the last description, he looked a lot like that giant of yours, bub."

The car started to move. "Just a warning," he hissed. "For your own protection. And if my old lady dies, I'll be back with the law, you hear!" He drove off in a cloud of dust.

Speaking of driving off, what's that I hear out my window? Hold it a minute.

• •

Guess what just happened? Dad was trying to leave the circus — on wheels.

146

All our circus wagons are really trucks, you know. They each have their own peculiar motor sound. Papouli's (driven by Mamouli) roars. The garden truck Papouli drives gurgles. Mine kind of chuckles. Boomie's whinnies like a horse when it starts, though it grunts when it lunges up a hill and sighs on the way down. The Solomons' (driven by Bimba) gives off an appropriate chatter. The engine of Polyphemus's wagon sounds like Tibetan chants or a lathe turning wood. But the engine I heard start up a while ago was the animals' truck Bimbo drives. The big old motor growled and snorted the way it usually does, but there was a horrifying shriek coming out of it too. I dashed over. Dad was in the driver's seat. The key had been left in the ignition, and I think he would have driven off with all the lions if he had known how to release the emergency brake. That's what was shrieking.

When I pulled open the truck door, Dad didn't argue. He just swung down meekly and went to sit on his haunches under a tree, tasting the engine grease on his fingers. There is nothing as sad as gorilla sadness. It is the most profound sadness humankind is ever likely to witness, when it really settles over that long, flat face. It makes me ache to have seen it on dear old Dad.

What could be troubling him so?

24 ✍

OH CHRIST! Oh Jesus! I hurt so bad! I'm wearing my bell cap to hide the knot on my head. I'm sitting in my padded clown pants to ease a pair of inflammations. I think I squashed a nerve in my neck. Never again will I attempt to levitate. I finally really made it, and I hate it.

I should have saved my act for Mamouli, but Papouli and Dad dropped by while I was practicing. The showoff in me blew the whole plan. Want to have a good laugh on me? Listen to this: I was seated there on the floor of my wagon and Papouli says, "Well, Bobby, how's the thigh-flapping coming along?"

"It so happens that I bumped all the way around the handball court yesterday," says I, "and my thighs were quite loose the whole time."

"Quite loose, were they? We'll have to see that to believe it."

"Okay," says I. "Maybe I'll give you a demonstration.

Just stand over there by the sink, shut your face, don't laugh, don't scratch your belly. We're putting the serpent to sleep, understand?"

"What kind of serpent is it?" he asks. "Dad's afraid of snakes, you know." And Papouli makes the gorilla sit up on the windowsill, where it's safe.

So I say, "You know perfectly well the snake's inside of me where she can't do any harm. And she's not really a snake, anyhow. She's symbolic."

"Those are the poisonous kind," he says to Dad, who lifts his feet, looking around the floor with a certain apprehension I can't help laughing at. Papouli leans an elbow on the gorilla's knee and yawns. I tuck my legs into a lotus. I close my eyes. I get serious. My mantra starts to hum along in a very businesslike way. It is a no-nonsense mantra this time, out to bore the absolute hell out of the kundalini. Before long, by golly, she's snoring away. But I decide not to take any chances. I'm going to make sure she's settled deep into a dreamless sleep before I give out my scream. In fact, I've somewhat dozed off myself, when suddenly Papouli lets out a hair-raising shriek that sends Dad flying backward out the window. I shoot up, slam into the ceiling. Wham! Headfirst into a half-inch-thick layer of plywood. My ears are almost ripped off, and I crash down on my butt. Thank God I'm well endowed, or I would have gone through the floor too. I look up through a haze of stars. In the spinning room the refrigerator door has flown open, and eggs are rolling one by one off the rack and falling with a splat onto the wooden stool upon which I sit at this moment describing the incident and wishing that at least it had happened in the tent where we would have had a paid audience. The poodles are huddled in the sink in a big terrified ball of fluff. Dad staggers up the steps.

"Well, I must say, Bobby boy," says Papouli, "they sure put one hell of a spring in your ass. If you teach that to Mamouli, be sure to have her do it outside. And have her wear a parachute and an oxygen mask."

Oh, then the hot words flew. I'm not supposed to be disrespectful, but I let him have it. I told him I didn't see any point in calling ours a great circus, when the big boss was only putting on a hypocritical show. "I don't care what you look like up on the wire. With your feet on the ground, you're a petty tyrant and a bully."

"Bully I may be," he growls. "But if you expect me to be impressed because you've learned how to hit the ceiling, forget it. I did that in high school, in the privacy of a locked room. You're infected, Bobby. She's infected you with her vainglorious desire to liberate herself from the fatness of her own flesh."

"You talk that way about your own wife," says I.

"How are we supposed to perform with the greatest of ease when everybody's caught up in this craving to leap out of his skin? We're a mystical circus, goddam it. We're supposed to be desireless out there. We're supposed to help people love and accept their condition and see the magic of it. We're not supposed to represent some kind of divine discontent."

"Even fleas," says I. "Even fleas in a flea circus get to hop when they feel like it." And Dad, hearing a word he recognizes, pulls a flea from his knee and sets it on his palm, and the flea leaps into Papouli's mustache and bites him hard on the lip. And it serves Papouli right.

25 🖋

"WHAT DO YOU see in there?" I asked, tapping the crystal ball Polyphemus was polishing.

"I'd just as soon not tell you," he said. "It's a rotten one. I'm not even sure it's worth trying to fix. In fact, if you want your fortune read, forget it. I lent my crystal ball to the guy who brought me this one. The balls up there on the shelf are worthless. I think I'll let Mamouli have them for a new juggling act she wants to try. That's what she was in here for just now."

Polyphemus has less to do than the rest of us, so a few years ago he set up a crystal-ball repair service. Gypsies drop them by, and Polyphemus is supposed to deliver them when we make the return circuit. But half the time the gypsies have migrated to parts unknown. He says he hardly ever gets a crystal you can make sense out of any more. They tend to develop a warped future because of transient radio and TV waves. About all he can do is clear them, polish them up, maybe round them off and balance them. But they don't last long. They lose their focus on the future in a month or two, then the customers write nasty letters.

"I'm about ready to drop this business," he grumbled. Our supposedly emotionless giant is just a bit insulted that Papouli took all the credit for having figured out the Lazarus act. He's been pouting for days.

"Mamouli was all excited when she danced out of here," I said. "She told me you read her fortune. I thought I'd ask if you'd read mine too."

"Are you kidding, Robert? I told Mamouli this was a busted ball. Don't tell me she took the reading seriously."

"That was my impression."

"Then I'm a boob and I'll have to go retract what I said. Doesn't anybody catch on to my sense of humor?"

"What made Mamouli let you read her fortune anyhow?" I asked. "I thought she put her trust in feeling. Crystal balls are brain oriented, aren't they? They're for mind reading."

"How many times have I told you, Robert? I don't read minds. I read feelings. Can I help it if feelings end up in the mind? If I had my way, they'd stay in the flesh where they belong. All they want to do is make war with our thoughts. That's why most of us are such neurotics."

"Not you, of course."

"Not me, Robert. My head's as clear as the Aztec Crystal. Though I wouldn't mind taking a vacation from this third-eye role. I sure would like to find some way up to the seventh, like Lazarus."

"Think he'll make it?"

"He'll make it. The question is, Will Mamouli make it?

152

If I was one to worry, I'd be very worried. From what I gather reading Dad's skin language, she's nothing but a mass of twitches."

"You wouldn't be quite so concerned," I said, "if you stayed up writing in your notebook as late as I do. Have you ever heard the Great Papouli Orgasm?"

"Can't say as I have, Robert."

"You must be a sound sleeper, Poly. Every night since Lazarus entered our camp. The lad's affair seems to have stimulated our chief. When he lets go, my windows rattle!"

"You're speaking in bad taste," said the giant.

I couldn't help myself. I started to giggle. Damn me! What is it about a grown man that still likes a dirty joke? I think I've hung around the roustabouts too much. I giggled myself sick in front of Polyphemus, feeling ashamed the whole time, while he looked down at me askance, polishing the crystal ball with a chamois rag dipped in his special homemade cleanser.

"He must really be balling her these days," I spouted, with tears in my eyes, immediately regretting the unfortunate choice of words as Polyphemus withdrew his hands from the crystal and scowled at me.

"You *are* a dirty one, aren't you, Robert? Perhaps you better leave."

"I'm going out for a picnic with Annie and Mamouli," I said. "Do you want me to tell her your reading was only a joke?"

"Do that."

"What did you say her future might be? Did you include the usual advice?"

He chuckled. "Oh, I said that if she wanted to walk on

air she'd have to become like an elephant. Sleep, eat, talk, walk, make love the way Annie does. I said that here in the ball I could see her growing bigger and heavier every day, as the image of herself as Annie's mate solidified. I saw her up on the high platform releasing the elephant image with a rapid flick of her mind. Out of the elephant flew the woman, in a burst of levity. The sudden change of weight sprung her into the air. Voilà! She's walking without a wire!"

I went to the door. "I'll tell her you were only kidding."

"Not me, Robert," he protested. "It's this ridiculous ball that distorted the picture."

"Can you see any truth in there at all?"

"Not really. Just a hint — badly out of focus. Not even the best crystal balls read the future, anyhow. All they read is future fancy."

"Well, what's my future fancy?"

"Come back over here, Robert," he said. "I can do it better with my hands. But if I see some vulgar performance by you, I refuse to look any further."

He wrapped his hands around my skull, cocked his head and listened. "You'll marry your poodles and live happily ever after."

Was that humor? Or was it envy? Polyphemus has always lusted after my poodles. He's always whistling for them, trying to get them to come up into his wagon. He'd just love to be able to stretch out at night, like me, in a pile of living, panting, hot poodle wool. I don't need a crystal ball to know that if he ever got my poodles, *he'd* be the one to marry them.

26 ✍

AT FIRST I THOUGHT it was Dad who tapped my
shoulder as I slept. I rolled over on my back and opened
my eyes. I could barely see his outline on this black
night, but a few of the poodles raised up to have a look,
and they seemed satisfied as they fell back to snoring
and twitching their paws, in the memory of some pre-
historic chase.

"You again," I said. "Why do you keep bothering me,
old fellow? It's not my fault. She'll be back in bed with
Papouli soon enough. A big strapping ape like you
should know how to take care of himself. Annie's taking
excellent care of Mamouli, if that's what you're worried
about."

He poked me with his finger again.

"People as close and as much in love as they are," I
tried to explain, "need to make space. Most arguments
between couples are just excuses they cook up for that

purpose. Why they don't just make the space to begin with — "

"Thou hast," he interrupted in a solemn voice, "caused the Great Mamouli to go sleep with an elephant."

Such Biblical language — in fact, any language at all — set me straight that I was dreaming, which made me wonder whether I *was* dreaming, because I'd never known I was dreaming in a dream before. In any case, I realized this was not our dear old Dad who squatted before me, but someone much more majestic. "Who are you?" I inquired.

"They call me the Great Grand-Dad. Companion to the Great Grand-Papouli."

"Pleased to meet you, I'm sure." I felt a flutter in my right ventricle. "How fares our patriarch?"

"He fares frivolously," said the Great Grand-Dad. "I am come to speak on serious matters."

My eyes had grown accustomed to the dark, and now I saw the gorilla open a briefcase beside him and remove a sheaf of papers.

"Frivolously?" I said.

"He squanders his days at play with the child Mozart. Musical billiards and blow-bottle music. They frequent the celestial taverns challenging Haydn and Christian Bach to matches of spitting at the rims of gold spittoons — to make them spin. They are courting the recapitated Madame de Pompadour, or is it Marie Antoinette? I can't keep track of these silly affairs. I myself am engaged in a major effort of our race."

The Great Grand-Dad lifted his arms. I was amazed to see that there were webs between his feet and his hands. The stretched furry surface gave him the shape of a

156

huge, winged bat. "While the Great Grand-Papouli and his newfound friend disport themselves, behold, Robert, known as the Grip: We, the demeaned ancestors of your questionable tribe, are at work full-time evolving. While you tinker with machinery, our aim is to bypass you within ten years, and then to reappear on earth as creatures of flight. No time to waste. Therefore, I shall read thee this stern warning, and be on my way." He held out the papers and read:

"Thou, Robert Grip, art an interfering fool, a bounder, a scoundrel, scalawag, rogue, clown and meddlesome mischief-maker. Cease and desist giving advice, or next time I shall appear in my fearsome role as the Great King Kong. I shall pick thee up in my fist, like one of those lizards favored by your dangerous friend Beauty the Midget, and I shall hold you atop a skyscraper, squirming in the air, while the depraved mob of moviedom, gorging itself in the pit, screams for me to gobble you up; for 'twas you and you alone who persuaded Mamouli to pack her bag and to go live with Annie the Elephant. 'Twas you who caused the forlorn sadness of my good, kind ape called Dad."

The Great Grand-Dad stuffed the papers back in his briefcase and leaned forward to speak less formally. "Dad can't bear dissension, Bobby. He's miffed at Papouli right now. He's giving him the cold shoulder. He thinks Papouli's the one who sent her away. How would you like him to find out it was you? Give any more advice to Mamouli or anyone else, my hairless friend, and I'll have words with Dad. Do you fetch my meaning?"

Hearing his name, Fetch awoke and barked at the Great Grand-Dad, and our patriarch's patriarch was gone.

"Yes sir," I said, hoping he could still hear me, out there. "Forgive me. Nobody's ever taken my advice before, don't you see? I would never give it if I thought anybody was going to take it."

I'm afraid my excuses didn't catch up with him. But what the heck, dreams are only dreams. They belong to me, don't they? To *my* imagination. I can make them or break them at my pleasure. I will not be incriminated — oops! I will not be *intimidated* by the mere shadow of one who has passed on. I declare here in the brightness of day, as I sit on a rock overlooking the valley, where, far in the distance, I can see Mamouli and Annie gamboling among the wildflowers, that I find their love affair beautiful. They are females in love.

Since Mamouli went to live with Annie they have become inseparable friends. They hike out to the country every morning now. Both have a passion for wildflowers. By gathering them, they've found another way to express their passion for one another. I don't care what my dreams tell me. I'm glad they're together.

Mamouli loves Annie for letting her fly off on long, exhilarating astral journeys. Annie wraps her trunk around Mamouli at night and gathers her close into her warm belly. I've peeked into the elephant pavilion and seen them there in a slant of moonlight, so tranquil. Mamouli fulfills Annie's most extravagant erotic fantasies. While Papouli may have ceased to see Mamouli as voluptuously exciting (to put it plainly, he thinks she's too fat), Annie weighs a ton and a half for every hundred pounds that Mamouli does. Mamouli must seem a petite, rosy little runt of a thing to our elephant; a dear, tender, perfect darling she just can't get enough of cuddling with. Beauty and the behemoth stroll through the meadows shoulder to shoulder, swaying in slow rhythm while Annie's trunk sweeps the tops of the flowers, curled at the tip, sucking in the scents; and Mamouli's arm swings down too, as she gathers flowers into the bouquet she will carry when she enters the arena in pink leotards, on Papouli's arm, reunited with him in public (where all things are redeemed) for the opening parade.

In my opinion, though Mamouli has become unmistakably more like a pachyderm in the seeming heaviness of her movements, this has only increased her human loveliness. It's done her good to quit the act on high. While Papouli put on a show of being hurt, I could see that he was actually pleased to have a chance to go back to the propeller helmet he and the twins have been wanting to get out of storage and fool with some more.

Mamouli intends to stay out of the tent while Lazarus does his Greatest Fall on Earth. I think that's wise and fair. Whether she's jealous because Boomie's the one who gets to call him back from the dead, or whether she genuinely fears for the safety of Lazarus, she just doesn't have any faith in that act yet. She will, once she sees how well it works out. She'll stop wanting to one-up Lazarus, too, now that Papouli's giving her more leeway with her other acts. He's accepted the snipping of the marionette strings. He's replaced Boomie with Mamouli in the dolphin-tank act (so Boomie can get ready for her new part in the finale), and he has the twins working on a cable thick enough for Annie to walk on. Without having to appear in the finale herself, Mamouli can give more energy to the act I know she's still working on. (You know the one I mean.)

27 ✍

ALL EYES ARE RAISED to the highwire gone berserk. The blade that was spinning so smoothly on Papouli's steel helmet now whips and dips, almost tearing his head off. Bimbo and Bimba, who had been whirling so nicely at each end of the blade, wobble in their orbits until it seems the swivels attached to their belts at the back are bound to snap and fling them into the crowd. Everybody draws in a deep breath and holds it for dear life. And look! Papouli finds his legs again. He's calming the wire. It's coming under control. The blade begins to whir smoothly again, like a propeller. The twins are spinning, blossoms of blue and pink. The audience lets out a great sigh. Papouli is lifted up lightly from the wire. For a moment he treads air, then settles softly on the tips of his toes and springs again. Parents and children settle back, delighted. And now they laugh with anticipation. Here comes the white-faced clown who smiles whenever he falls. What's he going to fall from now?

A whistle from above. Lazarus looks upward. The propeller has stopped turning. The twins unfasten themselves and hang by their hands. They handwalk to Papouli, walk up the wire to opposite platforms and slide down the ropes. Papouli lifts the blade from his head, drops it with the helmet to a net I've set up. I carry the paraphernalia away. The twins walk over to Lazarus and speak to him.

What? he says, pointing up to Papouli who gestures to him. He wants me on the wire? Nothing doing. Papouli whistles again. The twins nod vigorously. Yes, he wants you. Hurry up. They walk out of the tent. Lazarus puts his fingers deep into his mouth and looks wide-eyed at the crowd, then up to the gesturing Papouli and back to the crowd. What does he want with me? He wants you on the wire, the kids shout.

Lazarus pokes a finger into his chest. Who? Me? He looks to the ground and steps onto an imaginary wire. He loses his balance, jumps off, throws the back of his hand to his brow and staggers about, almost fainting. Me, with my vertigo? He marches toward the crowd with a horrified appeal in his eyes. He points his thumb over his shoulder. Go way up there? Are you kidding? Don't you remember how I fell off the trapeze and nearly killed myself?

To the wire! To the wire!

Lazarus climbs to the wide wooden railing and tries to walk the flat surface. He slips and falls into a lady's lap. The crowd roars. He gets back up on the rail while Papouli whistles for the third time. People in the front row

161

jump out of their seats and stand aside. Lazarus loses his balance, flips backward through the air and lands neatly in a vacated chair. Applause. People are on their feet now, trying to see. He rushes up the aisle to the young woman wearing a silver kerchief. He jumps into her lap, throws his arms around her neck and begs her to protect him. Papouli looks down from the wire and beckons sternly. Lazarus sadly stands, bids the woman farewell, kisses her hands, her cheeks and, ardently, her mouth. He sighs and sets forth with resolution.

In the Sun Ring he leans back, looks up warily. He reaches under his white leotard and pulls out a scarlet handkerchief from the region of his heart. He covers his mouth and coughs repeatedly into the handkerchief, then puts it back and pats the place where it covers that sickly organ.

The crowd grows impatient. To the wire! To the wire!

Lazarus throws back his shoulders, strides boldly to the rope ladder and seizes the bottom rung. He tries to pull himself up, hasn't the strength in his arms, manages to get a leg through and drags himself up that way. But the ladder wiggles when he stands on it. He can't seem to get it under control. The crowd urges him on with hoots and applause. He looks over his shoulder anxiously, eager to please, and throws a kiss to his beloved. She stands, unfastens the kerchief, lets the coat fall from her shoulders. Her flaming hair tumbles over her body. Everyone gasps to see that it's Boomie.

Boomie the Boomerang Lady is seated among them. She's the one he loves! Again they stand to have a look, and then nobody can see. They gradually persuade one another to sit, so everybody can watch her wave her silver kerchief toward Lazarus, who makes a more valiant try now. Look, he's climbing the ladder.

I, the one-man band, sit before an imaginary electric organ. I pull out one of the stops and play a baritone sax rendition of "Jacob's Ladder." The audience joins in, singing and humming. The pilgrim continues his upward climb, shaking in every limb, while the great father on the wire waits, frozen in perfect balance.

See Lazarus, amazed at himself as he stands with shaky knees on the platform. He sticks his neck out, pulls it back, looks to heaven, blinks his eyes pleadingly. The stern Papouli's hand reaches back and circles in a slow, insistent gesture of invitation. Lazarus looks downward. He spots me standing by the rolled-up net. Unroll it, he signals. I shake my head. Mr. and Mrs. Solomon, sitting on the net with their arms over each other's shoulders, shake their heads too.

Go! Go! Go!, shout the children.

Lazarus places a slippered foot on the wire. The foot slips forward. He lurches back, grabs a rope. He shakes his head. The crowd laughs, then roars its demand.

He points to his chest. What is this? Do you want my blood? My heart — see? Very weak.

Lazarus walks forth. One step, two, three . . . his arms out stiff, they tilt. Look out! He's on one foot. He begins to fall. Women shriek. His hand catches the wire. He dangles there, throws a leg over. Women take their fists out of their mouths, children ask if they can open their eyes, men fold their arms tight over their chests. Look, he's back on the wire. He pulls himself up. He's walking again. See how he staggers, lurches, slips forward, stretches out his hand toward the backward reach of the old man. He's almost there. He's going to make it. A few last quick steps and . . . careful! He's leaning way back, his arms flail the air. Laughter. He'll make it, don't worry. This is part of the act. This clown is a good one. See how he flings his torso forward at the last instant. Boomie isn't worried. The beautiful woman is among us, seated in calm radiance, confidently watching.

The tips of Papouli's fingers now touch those of Lazarus. A ripple of giggles. That was scary, wasn't it? *What?*

My God, he's falling! The whole world screams. Lazarus strikes exactly at the center of the Ring of the Sun.

The body of Lazarus bounces high in a cloud of sawdust. It turns, lands him on his face, he bounces again, revolves, lands on his back again and lies still. There is not a sound in the tent. Everyone stands in helpless dismay. Papouli remains on the wire, gazing upward in horror as if unable to accept what has happened. The apes squat against the poles, weeping. I rush to a microphone and ask if there's a doctor in the house. A gentleman (a genuine doctor known to everyone in the town) rises from the stands and hurries down. Bimba, disguised as a nurse, gallops in on Pegasus, carrying a medical bag. The doctor and the nurse kneel beside Lazarus. The doctor pulls a stethoscope from the bag and listens for a heartbeat. The crowd listens with him. He shakes his head.

Meanwhile, Boomie, dressed in scarlet, descends slowly from the stands. She opens the gate at the rail and steps onto the track. In a kind of trance, she enters the ring and kneels between the nurse and the doctor. She drapes her long hair across the dead man's body and lays her head on his chest. You can hear the sobbing in the audience. Boomie lies completely still upon her lover. Presently she raises her head and speaks to the doctor. She puts a finger to her lips. The mourners become hushed once more. The doctor again places his stethoscope on the dead man's chest, while Boomie, her forehead against the ground, speaks into Lazarus's ear. The doctor cocks his head. What's this? The nurse, with a downward motion of her hands, signals the crowd not to stir. Does the doctor hear something now? He takes hold of the limp wrist. Yes. There's a faint flutter. He listens again with his stethoscope. Boomie clenches her hands and speaks fervently to the one we can now see she loves with all her heart. The doctor stands, looks about with astonishment as performers and animals rush toward him. He speaks to us excitedly. We embrace, fling hats and masks into the air. The fool's alive!

As if waking from a dream, Lazarus sits up, rubs his eyes. He smiles wanly at Boomie as she bends toward him with open arms. Pushing her gently away, he places his hands on the ground, raises up, falls back down; then, with fierce determination, gets to one knee and reaches to us for help. We pull him to his feet. He thanks us, but shoves us off as we try to restrain him from walking. On weak legs, he stumbles to the ladder. I hurry to man the spotlight, and follow him with it as, struggling five rungs up and three rungs down, ever more valiantly, he attains the platform. The transfixed Papouli, still balanced on the wire, comes to life, feeling a vibration underfoot. He turns to see Lazarus walking shakily toward him. Nobody laughs now. Lazarus reaches out plaintively. Papouli rushes to him, grabs him by the wrists, steadies him, slips his great hands down to the slim waist, lifts Lazarus high up and around, sits him on his mighty shoulders.

He who fell from on high throws out his arms. The smile of smiles breaks out upon his triumphant face. Boomie, below, throws him kisses. With a roar of elation, the crowd rises as one.

28

WHY DO THINGS always have to go badly just when they're going especially well? It happens so often, the answer must be obvious. But it escapes me. Mamouli says we're trying to restore the old body the old way, and that won't do. We must be more bold, make a great leap of consciousness. Maybe she's right. She seems to be after something too radical, though, for a conservative like me. The twins say not to panic. We can still keep the balance. But Fetch is on the defensive, and that influences me. He keeps his poodles herded now, won't let them go over and visit with the lionesses. His growl indicates a suspicion of conspiracy.

Ever since Calypso stuck his nose in a corner again, Fetch has been worried that he's going to be put through the same ordeal. The lionesses told our lion that he'd have to choose among them, you see — at least that's what Polyphemus reads. Fetch isn't about to risk losing his harem. I guess it's wrong. I know it is. But I support him on that. I'm his best friend, after all. They're my harem, too, in a perfectly decent way. I mean, I sleep with them. I lie among them. Okay, I love them, that's the truth, but not in the way Fetch does, of course. Fetch wouldn't understand a Platonic relationship. He's plenty passionate and jealous. He doesn't want to go catatonic like Calypso.

Let me tell you Calypso's history, and you'll see how sadly circular it has become: Our lion was a real king in Africa; of that I'm sure. We have papers on him. He was captured over there in his early prime, shipped to our country and sold to a county park, where he was stuck in a cage that was much too small. The caretaker, who knew nothing about lions, overfed him until Calypso grew so fat he couldn't even pace about. That's how we found him — stuffed in a cage, glassy-eyed and so despondent that when we paid for him and took the cage out to our circus grounds and released him, he just lay there for a long time. Then he stood up and walked out of the cage to a place where two wagons came together at an angle. He stuck his nose in the wedge and stood with his rump to us, his tail between his legs.

Our six lady lions put up with this for a few months — wherever we went, he'd just stick his nose in a corner and stand there — then they raped him. I can't remember who was in heat at the time, but with their jaws the others dragged him into the position they wanted him in, and Calypso got raped. After that, he did fine. He became his old African self again, until the other day when his six wives decided they didn't want to share him anymore. According to Polyphemus, they let him know they each loved him, but if they couldn't have him for themselves alone they were either going to give up sex or hold out for a lover all their own.

Papouli blew up when he saw our poor troubled lion trying to make up his mind. He blamed Mamouli's cutting of the marionette strings for having inspired them to this folly. It was a sad day, he yelled at her, when the feminist movement began to infect the animal kingdom. The next thing you knew, every chicken would be wanting her own cock, every cow her bull. There would be a zoological crisis of the first order. And just when people were beginning to arrive again in caravans from distant regions, to see all seven parts of our circus body being played again. "You've got all the female animals puffed up with pride," he said.

"Animals need their pride," she answered.

"Aha!" said Papouli. "You admit it. A lion needs his pride."

That was a good one. He caught Mamouli off balance, and we all had a good laugh watching her sputter for a comeback. But you see, none of us really believed that stuff yet, about Calypso's pride rebelling. Today, however, it sure enough happened. Polyphemus called us to come see.

The field between our wagons and Boomie's is sometimes used for baseball. Calypso was seated on his haunches on the pitcher's mound. The cats lay in a yellow circle under a tree. One lioness at a time would slink out to the dusty gray circle of home plate, turn facing away from Calypso as if looking up into the stands, and flick her tail enticingly. If Calypso had known how to throw a baseball, we would have had a comic act to rival that of the famous Joe E. Brown. We didn't laugh, though. (Never laugh at a cat.) And what followed was really beautiful.

After she had lifted and fluffed and flicked and arched her tail for our lion, the cat in the batter's box would suddenly flop on her side and begin to roll back and forth in the most provocative way. What followed can only be compared, in my memory, to the closing night of the Follies Burlesque, which I watched backstage with Boomie and my father when I was a boy. Six of the greatest strippers in the world performed, followed by the one and only true saint of that art: the divine Lily St. Cyr, performing on her famous silken couch at the very back of the stage, between Greek columns — the temple virgin being deflowered by the invisible lover, who descends from above to raise her up arching in ecstasy toward the crescent moon that gleams down upon her pale and perfect flesh. That was the night Boomie broke my heart by claiming to see in that theater a vision of her holy destiny. It was the night my father spread out his baggy checked pants (the ones I wear now) on the bed of the hotel room and, laying his fake banana and his long false nose in the crotch of them, rolled them up and put them in mothballs and went to live in Florida. But I digress.

The cats!

Cha-Cha, Samba, Rhumba, Conga, Raspa and Bamba each took a turn doing this kind of striptease for Calypso, while he sat with paws planted firmly, front legs stiff, mane flying in the wind, looking slightly to the right so he could watch sideways with his left eye. I should check out our current astrological conditions with Bimbo and Bimba. Perhaps all the planets are finally lined up and our six lionesses came into heat simultaneously. Anyhow, when the show was over they lined up in a row along the first-base line and waited for Calypso to select the one he wished to share the rest of his life with. The poor fellow simply could not choose.

We watched and waited while he looked at each of his adored lionesses with that huge, pleading, sideways eye. Then he walked off toward the place where the Papouli wagon corners with the dressing-room trailer. He's been standing there ever since, with his nose stuck in the wedge, except when Polyphemus drags him out to perform. The lionesses didn't expect this. They stand around in a circle now, touching noses, consulting. Sometimes they trail into the elephant pavilion . . . who knows why? To get Annie's advice, or Mamouli's. Boomie's been going in there too. Our females are up to something, that's for sure.

What's that sound I hear?

It's Boomie on the steps of her wagon, sharpening her blades with a whetstone. She went off and started doing that back when we were on the baseball field watching Calypso walk away. The sound of the grinding gave an eerie feeling to the Mamouli-Papouli argument.

"See what you've done?" Papouli said. "You've broken that lion's pride."

"They're not *his* pride, I tell you."

"Then who the hell's pride are they?"

"Their pride belongs to them, stupid," Mamouli said. "They're their own pride."

"Their own pride, is that it? Listen, sweetheart. I don't know what you're up to, but instigating a rebellion at a crucial time like this is treason. We finally have this body together, and you want to break it."

"*Who* wants to break *whose* body?" Mamouli glanced

protectively toward Lazarus, who was walking away from the argument and going to join Boomie.

"Our body," Papouli said between clenched teeth. "You're going to break us all, just because you don't get to be our glorious rising sign." He cast an appealing glance toward the twins. "Ask your own children. You're out to destroy the balance, sweetheart. Tell her, kids. Tell her she's going to send us crashing if she doesn't stop inciting every female in this circus to cut the connection."

"Damn the connection! Why don't you lift up your eyes? We can't cling to the old body any longer. The times are changing."

"The times they are a-changin', are they?" Papouli put his hands on his hips and, leaning back, wagged his head. "That's a brilliant insight. Where did you ever come up with such a clever line?"

"Just another of the platitudes you taught me," she said. *"Sweet* heart!"

We laughed with her, for a change, and that's the only reason Papouli got carried away and told her to drop dead. He didn't mean it, and Dad shouldn't have reacted by throwing his shit at him.

• •

One summer of my late teens I sailed with my father from Florida to the shores of Costa Rica, where we entered the jungle on a parrot hunt. The monkeys followed us through the trees, flinging their shit at us. They laughed themselves sick. But let me tell you, for us on the ground there was no place to hide, and it wasn't funny.

Nor was it funny when, right in front of all of us, our gorilla, who has always been impeccably polite even when drunk, reached behind himself and threw a handful at Papouli. I will not disgrace you here, old man, by saying where you were hit. But we were not just shocked, we were stunned into an afternoon of silence and solitary reflection. Some good may come of it. Who knows but what Mamouli and Papouli have been so chastened that they'll never argue — at least in front of the family — again.

After throwing his shit, Dad turned his back on all of us and loped off toward a hillock in the distance, where he sat silhouetted against the gray sky, brooding.

A brooding lion. A brooding ape. That's bound to lead to a brooding Papouli. And Bob the Grip is brooding too. Some memory keeps trying to push up into consciousness.

29 ✒

I COULDN'T BELIEVE I heard Papouli sobbing. But it
was him, all right. I went over to see what was wrong.
Dad was away somewhere. When I climbed the steps of
his wagon, I saw that Papouli was kneeling at the foot of
the bed, praying to his image of the Virgin of Guadalupe. I didn't go in. For a while — just long enough to
make sure he was okay — I listened.

"I miss her!" he wailed."I miss her so much!" And he
went on sobbing like a little boy.

I was touched. I had had no idea he could lose control
that way. I wished Mamouli could have heard him. My
impulse was to run to Annie's pavilion and plead for
Mamouli to go back and be the good wife again. But I
decided to stay out of it. I've interfered enough already.

The Virgin of Guadalupe has always been Papouli's fa-
vorite. She stands on a crescent moon, rays of sunlight
like blades of knives around her body, her robe parted
sinuously at the center. There's a crown of stars in her

hair. Papouli once told me that she was originally a vaginal image drawn by a clever Indian who hoped to seduce the church into retaining the ancient cult of the black goddess, portal of fertility, receptor of corn, queen of earth. Her hands are clasped inside the deepest folds, shaping the sexual entry. Her face is hidden in the clitoral hood.

Sometimes I wonder if Papouli doesn't secretly worship Mamouli, and if his lording it over her isn't just for show. She's the source of his rebirth, after all. He wouldn't be the first man to torment the one he worships.

30 &

EVER SINCE DAD flung dung at Papouli, something in my past has been nagging me. I woke up just now and flashed on what it is! If this just had to do with me, I wouldn't bother to get up and write about it. But it has to do with Boomie and her father, so I must. I had forgotten a crucial reprimand her father gave me. He influenced me tremendously. He was like a vision of God come to earth. I guess I'd have to say he was even more that way than the Great Grand-Papouli, because he appeared earlier, when my soul was most susceptible.

• •

During my boyhood I sometimes traveled with my father on the burlesque circuit. But the stuff he did on stage made me ashamed, and while I was secretly fascinated by the stars of striptease, I was troubled by the crude familiarity my father displayed toward the women he pained me by calling "the cunts in the chorus." Those chorus girls were nice to me. They talked back tough to Father, and he deserved it. In front of him, they always made sure to ask about my mother. I loved her and lived mostly with her in a small town with tree-lined streets where nobody even knew I had a father.

We didn't have much money, so I had to get up every morning before sunrise, pedal my bike over to the newspaper office, gather my stack of papers fresh off the printing press, stuff them in two big white canvas bags that I hung from either handle bar, and pedal off to deliver my route, racing back home with just enough time left to gobble down my breakfast and pedal off for school. I loved it! Shall I boast? I was the most famous paperboy in the state. I won a gold plaque from the Lions Club for paper-throwing. They didn't call me Bob the Grip in those days, though they could have because the way I gripped the paper was the secret to my control. They called me Winger. Winger the Turtle. (The *Turtle* had nothing to do with anything except that my last name's Tertullian.) Looking back on it, I'd say I was what you might call a Zen paperboy. Sometimes people got up early just to watch me throw.

If you think Papouli can ride a bicycle on the wire, you should have seen me pedal no-handed down the streets with my slow, easy motion, my butt gripping the seat while I reached into a bag, whipped out a paper, snapped it into my special triangular fold and let fly to the houses on either side. I wasn't one of those goof-offs who make papers land in the bushes or even on the lawn. I put it exactly where it was meant to be.

I could make a newspaper land neatly wedged between two milk bottles, I could drop it to the center of the welcome mat, and sometimes (when I was lucky) I could stick it in the mail slot. I could sling a newspaper so that it slipped off the top of the roof, swooped across the back yard, out of my sight, and landed on the porch of the little rented cottage where an amazed granny always had a bag of toll house cookies saved up for me on collection day. I could make a paper curve around trees or swerve up a driveway and settle on a kitchen step. I could easily make one fly up to the second floor, zip into a window left open for me, and land at the foot of the editor's bed. I could hit the basement window of the woman they called "the campus widow" (though our town had no campus). More than once I waked a sailor in her bed, scaring him into a desperate tugging on of his impossible pants. I was the best-tipped paper-boy I ever knew. Nobody understood why I suddenly quit throwing. Here's why . . .

• •

I belonged to a gang. This was when I was already in junior high, I think. Anyhow, on sunny days we used to run for our bikes right after school and head for the vacant lot. Baseball was our game. What we liked to do was shag flies and grounders. Whoever had his turn at bat always stood in a circle of dust right in front of the boarded-up shack at the back of the lot. Besides being our backstop, this shack was also our clubhouse. We wrote oaths in blood on the wallpaper, hid our loot in the dried-up toilet bowl, and pantsed the crazy girl on the kitchen table.

One day we came wheeling around the corner on our bikes and discovered the shack door open. The boards had come down from the windows. A lady with a red shoe dangling from her toe was seated in a rocking chair on the front porch, strumming a guitar.

We leaned our bikes against a tree across the street and sat on the hood of a car, angry that someone had usurped our territory. We were already hatching plots on how to drive the lady away when we saw a little girl with long red hair bolt out of the shack, pounding her fist into a huge baseball mitt. She was followed by a lanky man dragging a baseball bat.

Before the man had reached the plate, the girl was positioned on the sidewalk thunking a fist into her glove and shouting, "All the way, baby, all the way, boy, all the way there, baby boy!"

The man swept the bat around in a wide, golden circle.

Up the ball whizzed into the stratosphere. It hung there, then zoomed down to where the girl stood with the glove at her belt. The ball popped in. She returned it with a leisurely one-hop toss. The man twisted around and snapped it up behind his back while the girl kept chattering, "Wayda go there, baby, wayda go there, boy, wayda go there, baby boy!"

After a while the man called out to us in a slow drawl. "Why donch'all move on in a little?"

We sprang right off the car and crossed over. We scattered ourselves about the lot, between the man and the girl. He started to hit us easy little pop-ups, signaling us with his long, bony finger to come in closer. When we were all feeling confident, he moved us back a bit. He kept moving us back that afternoon, until we were out there with Boomie (that's what her father called her,

179

though her true name was Boomer and his was Sooner).

All during school we thought about Sooner, and as soon as the bell rang we'd race for our bikes and head for the vacant lot, Boomie riding on my handlebars with her hair flying across my face. Sooner would already be there waiting for us, legs crossed at the batter's circle, leaning on his bat, looking up as if the sky weren't quite high enough for what he had in mind. The balls he hit kept getting higher and higher. He'd call out the name of the one who was supposed to catch it. The others spread out while the designated fielder ran all over the lot shouting, "I've got it! I've got it!" and the ball came down exactly where he'd been standing to begin with.

The balls Boomie's father hit were a thousand years old. They had the hides of a hippo. They were weary old heavy old waterlogged balls, but God Almighty how he could send them flying with his faded, long, yellow, swollen, narrow-handled, signed-by-a-champion, nicked and dented, rough-ended, plenty-splintered Louisville Slugger professional baseball bat.

• •

On a certain balmy afternoon, Sooner was hitting us flies when his wife — who often watched us from the rocking chair — called out, "Sooner, come awn insod. Ah gots somethin' nice'n hot in the ovin for ya."

She flounced into the shack with her guitar.

Boomie's father didn't pay her any mind. He started to hit them up higher and higher each time, while we took turns catching them and pegging them back to him on one fast hop.

"Sooo-ner," sang the voice inside. "You won't want it later. It's gonna get coooo-ler."

Sooner caught a throw-in, spat on the ball, rubbed it with his hands.

Boomie's mother was in the doorway now. "Come awn, baby. It's *mah* turn!"

Sooner put the bat behind him and kind of sat on the knob of it. He looked at us and he looked at her and he looked at the ball. Boomie ran in waving her arms.

"Not now, Maw!"

But she shooed her daughter away saying, "Go away, child."

Sooner tossed the ball up in a short little arc. He brought his body around in a tremendous wheeling of his thigh. He cracked the bat so fast all you could see was a blaze of yellow.

Up went the ball.

We watched it climb higher and higher. The ball was getting smaller and smaller, until it was just a white spot in the sky. Yet, small as it was, it covered the sun. When we looked up we saw it was locked in the center of a roaring fire, like the pupil of an astonished eye with light flashing out of it, out of a rip in the center of blackness.

The ball had turned black while the sun blazed out around it.

We stood there not moving, just watching, while the ball hung in the nest of the sun.

Suddenly we realized the ball was on its way down, roaring like a comet about to crash to earth. The ball was screaming with a cosmic rage that filled us with such awe that it was a long time before we realized we better get the hell out of the way.

We scattered in all directions, covering our heads with

our gloves, crying out warnings, finally closing up silent with our heads tucked under our wings.

Then we heard a sound.

Tat was the sound. *Tat!* Not like a ball hitting a mitt. But like a word. Like the first word of a child who sees that that and that and that . . . are that.

Tat. The ball hit Boomie's mitt.

We came out of hiding to find her there, with the ball like an egg nested against her belly. She was chewing bubble gum, one foot crossed over the other, the flap of her baseball cap turned back while she glared fiercely toward the shack.

Her father was no longer with us. The clubhouse door was shut. Boomie turned, walked across the street and slumped down under a tree. We watched her blow a huge bubble that she let burst upon her face.

We boys approached the porch. In the chalky dust of the batter's box lay the big, long Louisville Slugger. This was the first time Sooner had left it out. Usually he took the bat in with him when he was through. We walked up solemnly to the dusty pool, the solar circle in which it lay.

We lifted the bat, passed it around, slipped our hands over it, put it to our shoulders. Some of us tried a few cuts at the air, but we never picked up the ball from where it lay scarred and scabbed near a patch of crab-grass. Some of the lining was ripped off. The rubber twine showed through. Thick blades of flesh were peeling like sunburn from the blackened cover.

One of us threw the bat beside it and spat in the dust. We rolled the ball of spit around with the toes of our tennis shoes. Saying not a word, we walked across the vacant lot and crossed the street to stand near where Boomie was whittling on a twig with her jackknife. We put our arms around one another's shoulders and watched for a while. Then the others picked up their bikes, mounted them and, each in his own direction, wheeled homeward.

I stuck around until Boomie had finished whittling the stick and thrown away the stub. Then I asked her if she'd come ride with me on my paper route in the morning. She said "Why not?", and from then until I quit she sat on the handlebars, with her feet neatly crossed on the front fender, and I taught her how to throw so all I had to do was pedal and fold.

So, you see, it was I, alias Winger the Turtle, who got our Boomie started. Let me just tell you how her father got me stopped.

One day when I wheeled by to pick up Boomie, her father was painting the shack. He put his brush down, strolled over to me, slapped his hand down hard on my shoulder and said, real confidential, "You like throwin' that crap, Winger?"

"What crap?" I said.

"You like throwing all that crap at people's houses every morning?"

I didn't know what to say. I'd never thought about what was in the papers. Once in a while I'd look at the movie or sports pages. I wasn't partial to the comic strips, and I never more than glanced at what was on the front page.

Sooner reached into one of my bags. He started pointing to each of the headlines. "That's crap," he said. "That's more crap. That's still more crap, Winger."

When he had done this with just about every page, he closed the paper, jammed it back into my bag and said, in a voice that hurt me all the worse because it was so casual, so matter-of-fact: "You're teaching my daughter to waste her talent, Winger. Flinging shit."

He returned to his painting as Boomie rushed out the front door, eager as ever. She hopped up and we rode away. But I didn't deliver my papers. I took them out to the big rusty incinerator in the parking area of the highway department's maintenance lot, where the big yellow monsters were parked. I set fire to the trash in the can and was about to dump the papers in when Boomie told me to wait. She found a couple of bottles filled with gasoline or something and threw these in, to get a big bonfire going. Then she folded one of the papers. "Can you do this?" she asked. She threw the newspaper hard up into the wind. It circled over the bulldozers and flew right back to us, striking the side of the incinerator with a marvelous thumping sound.

We folded one paper after another and threw them until we could make them boomerang far out over the lot and back into the hoop of fire. The papers we didn't send into the fire got picked up and thrown again, until both of us had those papers circling in opposite directions and swooping back to thunk into the fire in perfect precision. When all the news had been consumed in flame, we hugged each other while the huge road machines watched, and I asked her to be my permanent girl. She said that suited her just fine, and we had regular dates that year her breasts were blooming. I gave her a gardenia every week, and once a month an orchid. I don't really believe this, because she's gone beyond me in every way, but the irony is that she might just possibly have stayed with me the rest of my life, if I hadn't suddenly decided one night that I was too good for her.

I, Bob the Grip, too good for Boomie. How do you like that?

What happened is that I made the mistake of taking her on the bus to the big city, to see my father in what was billed as the final night of the Follies Burlesque. Actually, it was a final night that ran for three more years before the show succumbed to pornographic films.

Boomie and I watched Lily St. Cyr from the wings. "It's like church out there," she said. She was so impressed that when the curtain came down she announced to my father that she was going to be a famous sex star some day.

This tomboy girl friend of mine said that to my nice but dirty-old-man father, without any shame. Pure little mama's boy that I had become, I was terribly disillusioned. Some silly ideal of what a girl should be had been violated. I stopped buying flowers for Boomie. I no longer took her to the drugstore or the proms. I became the center on the football team, and she became the state champion baton twirler, and we traveled to the games on the same bus. But we never even sat together. I was still in love with her, but I was stubborn.

One day the boys in my old gang told me they had made arrangements with Boomie to meet her in our old clubhouse. Her mother was away on a USO tour, and Sooner was off in the Pacific fighting in the war. She had told them we could have her all to ourselves for the whole weekend. She was going to show us some tricks.

You had to be tough about sex and manhood in front

of your pals, so I pretended I was eager as the rest of them, sick as I felt about it. She met us at the door on Friday night, in her mother's pink negligee and high spike heels, candlelight glowing behind her. I was the last one in the door. "I was hoping you'd come," she said.

But I couldn't. The word they'd used — "gang bang" — echoed repulsively in my head. I turned and walked away, across the lot, down the street and out of town, to the river, where I sat all night watching the black water and feeling the blood drain out of my heart.

I couldn't hang out with my gang after that. I didn't want to go to school or play football or baseball. I could see that the other boys had been changed in some way by that weekend — changed for the better, I would say now. I have no idea what Boomie did with them, but it put a serious look on their faces.

So I ran off and joined a carnival and then a circus, and I got so lonely that I finally wrote Boomie and asked her why she'd done that, and she wrote back and said she didn't know, but she hadn't done anything bad. All she did was initiate those boys. We started writing each other fairly regularly. She wrote a long letter when her father got killed by a hand grenade. I went home for the funeral, and we were friends again. Just friends. She became a rodeo rider, an exotic dancer, a pitcher on a girls' baseball team. Finally, I talked her into trying out for Barnum-Ringling, where she developed her first act as Boomer and Her Boomerangs. She spoiled me for other women, but I don't hold it against her. I'm one of those clingers to a boyhood memory, a boyhood passion. I have worried about Boomie as if she were my wife, but from a distance. Much as I've felt frightened and maybe even guilty, at those terrible times when she dismembered herself, much as I've suffered with her, I have to say that I'm proud to have taught Boomie how to throw. I'm proud that I'm the first one who kissed her.

How I do go on about my youth. But, you see, it all comes back to me now that in the eyes of her father, the man I most looked up to as the image of what I would like to become, I myself was nothing but a flinger of shit. And I guess I haven't entirely escaped that role today. So why should I feel shocked that a gorilla behaved that way, when at least *he* knew what he was doing?

31 ✌

Oops.

We've lost Calypso.

He vanished inside the twins' Black Hole machine.

Polyphemus doesn't seem to care though. I think he might even feel relieved that Calypso's gone.

The best the lady lions can do now is lie side by side at the entrance to the tent, letting people pet them or having children sit on their backs while their parents snap pictures. No sense in putting lions in a cage, when they've lost all interest in acting mean. They just lie there looking spiritually superior, like sphinxes staring into space. Once wild animals catch on to the mystical side of things, they can go into a kind of quietism that's positively obnoxious. They've been acting holy this way ever since the twins gave each of them a ride in their new carnival contraption.

We don't dare apply for a patent on the Black Hole now. The mistake, Polyphemus says, was for Bimbo and

Bimba to fit a time-space warp mechanism into it. We can forget about licensing unless Calypso shows up. For all Papouli's rantings and ravings, the twins remain infuriatingly confident. "Just a ballistic problem to be ironed out," they say. "The first airplanes that tried to break the sound barrier exploded in midair, and now we're on Venus. It took us ten thousand years to perfect the ax and less than half a century to get from heavier-than-air flight to flight in space. Human progress is accelerating so fast that we should have the mystical machines ready to balance the sexes and even launch Mamouli's walk on air, before this time next year. People would rather pet animals than watch them roar anyhow. For all we know, we may have warped Calypso back to the Garden of Eden. He might be lying down with the lamb, the dear old fellow."

"What are you talking about?" says Papouli. "If you're going to send people on a trip, you sure as hell better know where it is you sent them and how far back they went. And you better know how to retrieve them in time for the evening news. Most of our customers have to get up and go to work in the morning, you know."

Yep, he's miffed. The twins put the lionesses into the machine first, two at a time. The juice was turned on, off they whirled. There was a lot more noise than we expected, but not from the cats, just from the machine. When the ride was over they sat staring into space, as I said, perfectly content, as if they'd just enjoyed a vision of paradise and wanted to think about it for a good long while without any undue interruption. Their contentment has a quality of spiritual smugness that Papouli detests. They won't pitch in with the work. They won't growl or bare their fangs or do anything worthwhile. All they want to do — Rhumba, Samba, Bamba, Conga, Raspa and Cha-Cha — is lie side by side looking inscrutable. They snort contemptuously when you ask them to dance. They turn up their noses at meat. Who ever heard of vegetarian cats? Not that I mind. Rice and beans cost a lot less.

Nor do they seem to miss Calypso. They've been androgynized. I wonder what happened to him, anyhow. Maybe he's ceased to exist. Off he went for his hundred times around, sucked into blackness and blown back out into light. He got to spinning so fast we could only see a tawny blur. Then the blur vanished. We could see his seat spinning around with nobody in it. The twins were having a hard time getting the machine to stop. The control switch was jammed. I'finally had to turn off the main generator. Calypso must have done the figure eight at least a thousand times before he was erased. When the machine stopped, we found the safety belt still hitched. Since then, nobody's seen or heard of our old lion.

Where the devil could he be?

32 ✑

WELL, WHAT DO YOU KNOW? I said I wasn't going to
listen to a lot of complaining next time. I was going to
ask for a vision. And, by golly, not only did I ask for it, I
got it! This is going to be a very literary entry, with some
remarks by Mamouli that inspired me almost as much as
a sermon by the Great Grand-Papouli, in the old days
when he preached by the animal cages. Sometimes I
forget how bright Mamouli is. She can make Papouli
seem like a clown and me like a clown's footman. I think
her worries are unfounded, mind you, but her vision has
a stirring ring to it, and I, Bob the Grip, applaud the ex-
travagance of her paranoiac imagination.

Part of what she said was so beautiful that I had her
repeat it and I copied it down; now I'll have to lead up to
it in a worthy way. So! Ahem! To begin . . .

• •

I awoke with a start (as they say) when someone burst
into my wagon and sprawled across the floor toward

where I had been lying asleep amongst my dogs. I knew who it was even in the dark, by the smell of elephant dung and because the poodles didn't bark. They just began to whine while Fetch tugged at the sleeve of my pajamas. I lit a candle. Mamouli lay there sobbing. The poodles were all over her, trying to sniff out her trouble and comfort her with the caresses of their wet tongues.

I put on a pot of water for tea, then lifted Mamouli by the arm and sat her in my beanbag chair. I let her cry for a good long while, as I pulled the straw from her hair and tried to untangle the knots. Her skin was more crusted with dirt than mine has ever been, if that's possible, and her feet were caked with mud. I filled a basin with warm water, washed her feet, dried them with my pajama top, laid my head in her lap, and rolled my forehead on her knees and kissed them, while she clutched at my hair and wept and wept and wept.

When her tears were spent, I fixed her a big mug of Bob's Special Flowergrass Brew, and I made her sip it while I massaged her shoulders (thinking, when have I ever seen anybody give *Mamouli* a massage before?). She began to murmur a story about how Papouli was going to become a double murderer if we didn't do something fast, because he was bent on killing Lazarus by making Lazarus kill himself, and that meant Boomie would kill herself too.

"Impossible," I said. "We have to trust Papouli. We have to assume he knows what he's doing. He'd never do us any harm that wasn't for our own good, for our survival."

"But he *doesn't* know what he's doing," she said. "He

doesn't know he wants to kill Lazarus and he doesn't know he's in love with Boomie either."

"Then how do *you* know?" I asked.

"Because I lay up against him night after night and I felt the movements of his body, I pieced together words and cries. I put his dream together like a puzzle."

"What's in a dream?" I said.

"Plenty. Every night he leaves his body and goes off to a kind of battlefield. Did you know that? He goes off to slaughter Lazarus and attack Boomie."

"What do you mean, attack Boomie?"

"He rapes her."

"Mamouli," I said, and took away her tea cup and smacked her playfully on the cheek. "Wake up. It's *your* recurrent dream, not his. Even an amateur problem collector like me can tell you that. I've heard that some women have rape fantasies, but you must be the first woman to project the rape onto someone else."

She slid down in the chair and began to whine about how only she could remedy the situation, by taking on a role that Lazarus, with so little circus experience behind him, wasn't ready for; and how Papouli was jealous of her because he thought she was too spiritually ambitious, and all that other stuff. But I filled her cup with tea and handed it back to her, and then I clapped my hands once, loudly, right in front of her face, and I cried out, "Enough!"

"Enough!" cried Bob the Grip, catching himself quite by surprise with his tone of authority. "I want no more of this psychological bullshit. Give me a vision or go back to your elephant and leave me alone."

Mamouli seemed rather pleased by my firmness. I

went to get a rag, then wiped up the tea she had spilled and sat down beside her on my levitation mat and patted her knee and said, "Now. Talk to me like the *great* Mamouli."

We were silent for a long time, then she began.

"Every night," she said, "Papouli is the old king in his tent preparing to do battle with the young challenger. I stand close behind him buckling on his armor. I hand him his shield and his sword and he steps out of the tent into the morning sun. We are all gathered there to watch. The one-eyed giant, the prince and the princess, the brute, you the jester, all of us. We stand on both sides of a kind of alley like a jousting court with tents lined up. At one end, on a high throne, sits the Great Grand-Papouli in his judge's robe. At the other end, far across a field, Lazarus emerges from a solitary tent, with Boomie beside him shining pale in the sunlight like a prize. He embraces her. The two champions stride toward each other."

Mamouli's dream, or Papouli's . . . Mamouli and Papouli's recurrent dream enthralled me. I jumped up and hurried to get my notebook. "That's more like it," I said. "That's the way it should be told."

"It ends the same way every night," Mamouli said. "Lazarus falls. Papouli plants a foot on his body and looks toward the judge. The Great Grand-Papouli points his thumb toward the ground. Papouli plunges his sword into the breast of Lazarus. Blood rushes out onto the ground. Papouli throws aside shield and sword and lets out a cry of exultation."

Mamouli looked at me wide-eyed. "Shall I go on?"

"So that's the cry I've been hearing. Well then, the dream stopped when you went to live with Annie, because I've heard no more victory cries coming from your wagon."

"That's a bad sign," she said. "That means the killer's up out of the dream. Shall I tell you the end?"

"I can guess," I said. "Papouli goes to Boomie's wagon. He rapes her. Right?"

"Right," she said.

"I can see by the glow in your eyes that you like this story, don't you, Mamouli?"

She thought this over for a while and she said, "No, Bob, I don't like the story. But I like the level at which the story is lived."

"So do I," I said. "Why is that?"

We thought it over and talked about it there in the candlelight. Then she talked to me in a calm, very intelligent way that made me wonder why it is that outside the tent, in our day-to-day lives, we so seldom rise beyond a kind of tawdry, self-mocking performance — not just me but all of us, even the animals. I asked Mamouli about it and was so taken with her answer that I asked her to repeat it so that I could write it down word for word.

• •

Mamouli said: "Bob, I have never believed that the ordinary black and white newspaper reality is worth living — the world according to *Time* magazine and television. I've been inspired to perform impossible feats ever since childhood when my mother read me fairy tales. I believe what the Great Grand-Papouli believed — that we can truly be happy only when we put on our legendary masks and take on our mythic roles.

"I am a walker on air. That is how I see myself in my

dreams. If I believe that some day I'll transform that dream into a higher reality, then I have to give that same faith to my husband, horrible though his myth may be. I can only challenge the legend he dreams of fulfilling — the murder of the knight and the rape of the lady — with a legend of my own. I believe that we all have to find the courage to become our legendary selves, whether the legend be comic or tragic, solitary or bound to some mystical community. If Papouli doesn't awaken to a legend he can embrace, the way his father did, he'll never be able to embrace mine. Whether we're to become high priestess, hermit, fool, sorcerer, merchant prince, magician, clown, warrior king, or lady in heaven, we can't be satisfied until we join ourselves to a great tradition. Not just a recurrent dream. A recurrent *story*, in which we have played our parts in different costumes, in different tents, since before anyone remembers except in the memory of flesh. Being large, my body has always possessed a generous memory. It was the legend of the Papoulis that attracted me to the circus. I despise Papouli's petty behavior, and he despises mine. At that level, we're a crotchety married couple caught up in the endless battle of moderns to decide who defines the relationship. I welcome a more exciting battle, even if it drives me quite mad. I *want* Papouli to pick up the old king's mask his father laid down, even if it also means picking up symbolic sword and shield. And I mean to lift up his eyes to a vision of transfiguration before he ever has a chance to bury that sword in the body of the one he fears has arrived to dethrone him.''

• •

It's another day, and the magic of her words has diminished. But I copied them down all the same and have them here to reread and to restore myself with, on candlelit nights to come. Even now, as I prepare to pull on my overalls and go to get my shovel, I pronounce that I, Bob the Grip, Keeper of the Ground, am in awe of the great maternal beast who opened her mind to me last night and carried me down into the depths of her sea.

33

D AD IS DEAD.

Killed by Papouli in a battle we all watched without knowing how to stop it.

I can't write about this now. I'll try another time.

34 🦢

I KNEW THERE would be times like this when I'd have to write something down under pressure. I will not dissolve into a puddle of tears. Everything's ready in the tent. We are reaching a kind of climax. Three hours to showtime. Very well. Let what happens happen. It's my job to set the stage, and that's what I intend to do, nervous or not. Not nervous. My hand is steady. I'm here in the dressing room with the dogs, already made up and costumed, prepared, as Boomie's understudy, to take my chances when the time comes. I am somewhat trained to be everyone's understudy, though I'm a rusty one, I'll admit, since we've been in such good health until recently. But I wish *somebody* would show up. I can't do the whole show myself, for God's sake. Come on, Robert, get this notebook up to date, screw your courage to the sticking point, and save your tears for later.

• •

This all started when Annie came trumpeting in from the country in a panic. Mamouli wasn't with her. One look at Annie, and Polyphemus could see that Mamouli was in danger. "Listen," he said to Papouli, "you better get out there fast. From what I read on Annie's brow, Dad's trying to get her to jump off a cliff or something. He's telling her she can fly."

That's all it took. Papouli jumped onto Annie's trunk. She set him on her back and away they ran. I sprinted after them. When I reached the river, I saw Dad and Mamouli on the cliff above the opposite shore, directly across from me. Papouli was up there running toward them. Mamouli was crouched for flight, with Dad leaning on his cane puffing his cigar like an impresario, chattering with chin stuck forward, lips fluttering. He had on an old bowler hat Papouli used to affect in the old days. He didn't exactly push Mamouli. When he saw Papouli charging toward them, he just touched her with the cane. She kind of lost her balance. She didn't jump so much as fall. She fell down in front of me with a splat, right on the far side of the riverbank. The mud flew clear across the river and nearly knocked me over. I washed my face off as I waded across, and there she lay, not hurt at all, her entire body covered with the thick, pasty gray mud. By the time Papouli had run back along the cliff and down the path to join us, she was giggling hysterically. He knelt beside her. "Go away," she cried, flinging the mud off her arm at him. "We're practicing."

"Get up and come home," he said.

She looked up cheerfully toward Dad. "I forgot to release the elephant! I forgot to spring!" Then, to Papouli: "He has more faith in his little finger than you have in your whole body."

The gorilla leaned over the edge and twirled his cane. He doffed his hat to Papouli, then waved it as a signal for Mamouli to come back up and try again. Papouli snarled, struggled to get out of the mud, finally tore off his shoes and threw them aside, then took off after Dad. Both ran for the path, but Dad was so much faster that he had already reached the bottom and was splashing across the river by the time Papouli reached it. Off Dad loped toward our camp, stopping now and then to let Papouli almost catch up with him, then loping off again.

Since Mamouli seemed perfectly contented in her wallow of mud, I looked about for Annie, hoping to ride her back in time to avert disaster. I finally discovered her disguised as one of a row of boulders, farther downstream along the base of the cliff. She was lying on her stomach, not moving a muscle. She seemed to want to hide herself, vanish into the cliff. When I called, she gave no response. I left her there, hoping she'd come out of it and bring Mamouli back to us by showtime. Annie's such a responsible sort, I'm sure she'll respond when the time comes, if only by instinct — though my watch tells me she'd better hurry up.

Am I going to be able to tell this next part?

Dad and Papouli.

Wait a minute. I'm going to go feed an extra load of fish to Jack and Jill. I want to make sure they're well satisfied when I get in the tank with them.

• •

Dad and Papouli were already on the hill fighting savagely when I caught up.

I'm sorry. I think I'll just close the notebook at this point. I'll resume later. Much later. Come on, Turtle, stick your head out and face it. Don't be coy. If you don't, some reporter's bound to hear about it and put his distorted version in the papers as a "human interest story."

• •

Papouli was streaming with blood. He was streaming with blood. But he kept screaming for us to stay out of the way. When the dogs tried to get in there, he and Dad kicked them away. Even Fetch (bless you, friend) couldn't bring himself to bite. Those fat, female felines weren't any help either. They just lay in the circle licking their chops. But let us not blame them. Finally, Polyphemus came running with a gun he'd borrowed from a farmer. He wasn't about to shoot Dad, though. He handed the gun to me. I handed it to Bimbo, who tried to hand it to Boomie. We kept hoping they'd call it quits, shake hands and be friends again the way we'd seen it happen every night at the end of their wrestling act.

Lazarus put the gun in my hands again. Papouli was on the ground. Dad stood over him. I aimed at Dad's head. No, I didn't shoot him, because just then he did something that will always endear him in my memory. Dad put his hands behind his back, puffed out his stomach in a comic imitation of Papouli, and, while our chief staggered to his feet, he winked. Dad gave Papouli the Harry Houdini wink.

Papouli peered around at us through eyelids nearly swollen shut. Whether he saw us smiling with relief and clapping our hands, I don't know. But he heard us, and the sound put a grimace of such twisted rage on his face that our hands quickly dropped to our sides.

Papouli squinted directly at Dad's stomach, drew back his fist and threw a vicious punch to the solar plexus. As Dad crumpled over, Papouli struck him again right between the eyes. Our dear old gorilla dropped down dead.

There. I've told it. Papouli couldn't have seen the wink. I'm almost sure he didn't. But to have killed his own ape. Nobody should ever do that. Few of us ever find our ape and make peace with him. Those rare circus people I've known who understand the ape–human relationship will tell you that if you kill your ape, something horrible is bound to be released from the cage of your own breast. God knows, Dad was only trying to build up Mamouli's shattered confidence. Pity got the better of him. He was beginning to act too human, if you want my opinion. Some of you may think apes have only one direction to go when they die, and that's down. But I think it's time we raised the ape from the psychic underground. Therefore I wish my good friend, Dad, a flight with the angels up into paradise, and when he gets there I hope the greatest of all the Great Grand-Dads offers him first thing a big, long cigar.

• •

I see by my watch that we have one hour until showtime. What do I do now? Saturday's our big night. We're sold out and I can hear the mob at the gate already. I don't dare cancel. Some people drove three or four days to get here. We have to give them *something*. Polyphemus is letting them ride the cats. That should hold them for a while. The dogs and I are the only ones still in the dressing room. I shall keep on writing, to keep myself calm. Everything's ready to go, if only the cast would show up.

With Mamouli gone, Boomie took Papouli into her wagon to nurse his wounds. He's out of it. I stuck my head in earlier. He was unconscious on the bed, moaning. Boomie won't be able to make it for the parade. She'll do her finale and I'll cover for the rest. The twins helped throw Dad into the animal truck and then hurried off, troupers that they are, to work up something to save the show. They're going to disappear tonight, vanish in smoke through the hole at the top of the tent. I can count on them. Lazarus drove the body into town to leave it with a mortician. I wish he'd hurry back. I have to jump Boomie's motorcycle over the barrels. It's not that hard. I've done it. It's just that it scares the hell out of me. If I can't handle the dolphins, they'll figure out how to carry me around. We can turn the ride into something funny. Dolphins are at their best when they have to improvise. Where *is* everybody? I'm going to tie more ribbons on the poodles.

• •

A kid just arrived breathless on his bike, with word from Lazarus. On his way here, the kid says, he passed two chimps in sailor suits with packs on their backs. They were on the highway headed south. One was riding a little bike and the other was on roller skates beside her. They were traveling fast and not looking back. Who can blame them? I just hope they return some day. The Solomons were just starting to warm up to me. I was even thinking of working up an act with them and Lazarus, where we play poker using chips for cards and cards for chips. Damn it all, how often do you meet a really decent couple like that? I feel so rotten.

Come on, Bob, you feel fine. Be a rock! Once Lazarus gets back, the two of you can pull it all together. Lazarus told the kid to say he'd be here at the last minute. The people at the funeral parlor wouldn't handle an ape, the snobs. Not that they weren't perfectly happy to sell us an expensive casket. The man at the cemetery wouldn't give us a plot, either, but he lent Lazarus a shovel and showed him a spot just over the wall where he could dig. That's what our star's doing now. He's digging Dad's grave. And here's Annie with Mamouli. Good.

I'm not going to tell them about Dad. They both appeared too pleased with themselves when they looked in. I wonder what Mamouli did to bring Annie out of her funk. When I told them Papouli wasn't going to perform tonight and they'd have to come up with something special, they looked at each other with what I think the poets call "a wild surmise," and they positively lit up. Annie offered her trunk to Mamouli, and Mamouli linked her arm around it and off they marched to make their preparations.

I think we're going to get this night's show off the ground after all.

35 🦋

LOOK AT THE CROWD between the wagons and out there in the field. Look at the cars jammed into the old garbage dump far off to my left, their tops shining brightly in the noonday sun. Once again I have missed the beautiful moment. Once again everyone else has been transformed — in my family, in the town, in the larger mystical community. Sometime I'm going to figure out what it is about me that isn't there when it happens, or doesn't want to look, or can't, or refuses to look. God knows, I'm the very first to long for such a vision. Yet some moral force makes me hold fast to my position, and I remain on the outside here in my wagon, watching this Mamouli love-in take place on our circus grounds.

Tell me what it means. I don't know. So as not to spoil it for the others, I have mostly stayed by myself since Mamouli walked on air — how long ago? Has it already lasted for a week from last night, this hushed atmosphere of mystical festivity that I perversely refuse to surrender to, feeling all the time a certain spiritual shame or inadequacy? An obstinacy. Damn it! I can't fake it. I must feel as I feel. "If I am not myself, who will be?"

When I do go out, I let them hug me and smile into my face. I force a grin. I *want* to believe. I *want* to share. Yet, you see, I long for just a sign of sorrow from those people, too. And from the remnant of a family I'd think would be heartbroken. Some sign of remorse. We have lost our heart, haven't we? Haven't we lost her?

Just below my steps stand a man and a woman I have never seen before. They reach out for each other, giddy-eyed, repeating a scene that has become a common ritual among this ever larger gathering of the pious. They hold hands, draw close, hug and laugh, and over each other's shoulders they gaze up with adoration at the sky, draw back, still holding hands, and look at each other with watery-eyed rejoicing. Why?

Because they have seen Mamouli walk on air.

They, who loved her not at all. And I, who loved her so much and deserved to see her (read these pages and tell me that I didn't!) — I didn't see anything! Damn the conspiracy in the universe always to leave me out! What am I saying? Cross that out. Am I going crazy? Such vanity! A little bit of calm, as the Great Grand-Papouli would say. A little bit of calm, please.

Did I just curse God? No. Excuse me. Really. I love life so much. So many gifts. Such an abundance of joy. Thank you, God. Knock wood. You know it's just envy I'm feeling. I'm wondering whether I lack some kind of spiritual courage. I seem to be insisting on my grief.

Why is that? Because it belongs to me and I like it, like having it?

I never thought I'd see the day when the world became too miraculous for my taste. This whole event wants to shame me out of my sorrow. But, don't you see, without the vision my grief is my only connection to Mamouli, and I will not let it fly from me. There's something dreadfully disturbing about these sudden breakthroughs of bliss. Nobody had to do anything to receive them. No effort required, no discipline. All they had to do was stand there and hold hands and look up. It's a strange position for a circus person to take, I know. It makes no sense. I just can't stop asking myself why she appeared to them and not to me. I worked hard for that vision. I deserved it as much as anybody. Who believed more firmly than I did?

Between the wagons, hundreds of people stand about in rapture — adults with flowerchild smiles, children with the knowing eyes of old wise ones. Don't think I'm not in a certain sense grateful that others can believe. They make me feel inferior, that's the truth. Well, I *am* inferior. No, I'm not. I am, but I'm not.

I'm confused, that's the truth of the matter. I move between my own private sorrow and the bliss of those who surround me. If you were here, you'd understand what I mean. You'd feel intimidated. You'd feel spiritually inadequate for wanting to weep, and then you'd weep for not having the courage to weep, that's how crazy you'd be if you were in my place.

During my few sorties, I put on a good face. I pretend to share in the celebrations. I even go into the tent and hold hands and sway and sing and look up to that spot above the Ring of the Moon where she's supposed to be standing. But I don't see her. I pretend that I do, for their sake, yet something in me refuses. Could it be that I only loved Mamouli for *wanting* to walk on air? Maybe I just can't respond to her actually having done it. I mean, if they say she's done it, she *has* done it, hasn't she? Is the price you pay for having played the fool so long, that you don't get to be fooled by the greatest trick of all? The death-defying illusion? I'm beginning to think I'm attached to death in some perverse way. I must like the finality it gives to our lives.

The Great Papouli Circus has come to an end, my friends. It's finished, as far as I'm concerned. If you want to take pleasure in seeing our tent still filled with people day and night, go ahead. But there's no edge to anything, without an announced showtime, without an opening parade and a grand finale. They spill out of the stands, into the arena. They treat the Sun Ring like a sufi dance floor, the Ring of the Moon like the holy of holies. Bursts of spontaneous elation. Babble and laughter. Disorder. Dammit, Bob, can't you see they're right? Look up *spectacle* in your circus dictionary. From *spectaculum:* to sit as if in an augural temple. Mamouli has taken us back to our origins, dummy. Get with it. Dance with the others.

I'm cursed with the gravity of Newton, Papouli would say if he were saying anything these days besides "She did it, she did it."

Did she? Did Mamouli walk on air? How many really see her there still, and how many only pretend they do because they want to so badly? When one of us in the boyhood gang I wrote of earlier sneaked up to a window in the evening, crawling across the grass from behind a hedge, peeking in and returning excitedly with his report, he always claimed he saw a woman writhing on top of the covers, doing something sexy to herself. But when it was my turn to crawl to the window, she was always under the covers reading a book or snoring. I lied just like the others. I'm sure each of us wonders to this day whether he was the only liar in the gang. It's like that. Sometimes I think I'm the only one who didn't see Mamouli up there above the Moon Ring, shining down in a pole of blue light. Other times I'm convinced that none of us saw her or see her, and that I'm the only one honest enough to admit it. But I don't admit it to *them*, do I? Only to this secret notebook.

Who wants to be a spiritual spoilsport? Mamouli made them happy, that's the point. She amazed them. She only made me sad. What can I do but hide myself?

It's such a bright butterfly afternoon. The whole field is spread with families gathered around baskets and tablecloths. Bottles of wine catch ruby glints from the sun. Are those children trying to walk on air, or are they just trying to imitate the butterflies? Either way, it's not a bad thing to try. Maybe if enough people get it into their heads that they can get off the ground unassisted, somebody finally will. In their view, someone already has.

God, this is so disappointing. You'd think I'd be the very first one to get to see her walk on air. But when it happened I was decidedly looking down, and what I saw gave me no inclination whatsoever to look up. But others, who weren't there then, claim to see her now. That's the rub. If this keeps up, our tent's going to become a religious shrine. There'll be long lines of the lame, the halt, the sick and the blind waiting to get into the tent for a glimpse of the Great Mamouli. Could I lend my support to such a show? Mamouli pennants? Plastic Mamouli statues? Not on your life!

I feel lonelier than I ever have, except maybe for that time I sat by the river while the other boys did whatever they did with Boomie. Ironically, Boomie's my only consolation now. She's the only one besides me who didn't see Mamouli walk on air. She stays in her wagon too, compulsively sharpening those blades. I think she's going through the same turmoil I am — wanting to grieve, but not quite able to because of the resurrection atmosphere around here; yet not yielding to that either; refusing to mill about in the crowd the way Lazarus does. He and the twins and Polyphemus always have a mob around them. People like to touch them and look beatifically into their faces. Frankly, it makes me sick.

Papouli's out there too. But mostly he wanders off into the country, and I have to go bring him back at night. He's in a euphoric daze. He just keeps staring at the sky. Now and then he chuckles softly. "She did it," he says, when you take hold of him. "She did it. She did it."

I don't believe in his amazement. I just think he's trying to keep an illusion up in the air. He's juggling with a vision I don't believe he ever really saw. That's the curse of it for me. I can't believe in the reality of his experience. What is it in some of us that won't let life climax out of the ordinary, into the extraordinary? In self-defense I'd have to say our inability comes from a belief that the divine is precisely in the ordinary, and to leap out of what is common is to deny the revelatory fullness of our everyday lives. Whew! Well said, Robert. Scratch yourself a point.

A confession: I've never really caught on to either

Christianity or Buddhism. A major flaw, I suppose, for the one-man grounding crew of a mystical circus. Why would the divine enter human flesh, only to undergo excruciating suffering inside it, with the aim of finally achieving release and transcendence? With an attitude like that, why not just leave flesh alone? Leave it to those who love it. To people like me. Am I being a smart-ass, Papouli?

I love flesh, if you want to know the truth of the matter. I'm attached to it. Call me a spiritual cannibal. Even the flesh I held in my arms as we sped toward the hospital . . . screamed our way through traffic, while the others were gaping at another, fleshless, body that belonged to the same woman whose head I held in my lap: Even that stinking meat, bruised black and blue, is dearer to me than any insubstantial vision you might persuade me to see shining down from on high. I have never been attracted to images of saints. Not since I realized I'd lost my great chance at initiation because I'd made a teen-age saint out of Boomie.

What it comes down to, Mamouli, is that I wanted you to walk on air *in* the body — the real, solid, flesh-and-blood body. I'm mad at you, I'm very angry with you for not having done it that way. You took the gross beauty of your dear, petty, idiotic, warm, wonderful self away from me, and I will not make a triumph of it. Tomorrow, I'll tell in this notebook what happened here, as the others saw it and marveled. But I will not marvel. I will not see.

Bob the Grip refuses!

36 🖎

ONE ACT emerged easily from another, like a series of knots being untied, until the cord stretched so straight and tight and true that just the right note could have been struck, with overtones and undertones in perfect resonance, and our circus could have traveled on inspired as never before by the purity of purpose we longed to recover.

But we were perhaps too finely tuned that full-moon night. The final note was struck with such force that the world as we knew it snapped, spread into the vast silence of the universe and congealed into the image of a woman lifted like a goddess off the ordinary plane, shining down in motionless motion to guide the spiritual imagination.

This happened, remember, while the man who was the power among us lay wounded and confused and lusting, angry from the battle with his own shadow. "Such, too often in our day, is the condition of the men we choose to lead us," says Polyphemus. "Until their transformation, the time may have come when we again must look up to the greatness of the mother for our renewal."

I can't disagree. Yet I think the first half of the show was miracle enough for Mamouli to have performed. For me, her night of inspiration peaked sufficiently just before intermission. I would prefer to erase the rest, but I'm going to tell it all exactly as it happened.

• •

At showtime, we never would have guessed that Mamouli would come through so grandly. She and Annie were still off somewhere rehearsing. In the dressing room, Polyphemus, the twins, and I could hear the pounding of feet on the bleachers. But we couldn't seem to get our act together. We were still stunned by the death of Dad, angry at Papouli but worried about him too. He was in some kind of delirium, and Boomie didn't dare leave his side. We had decided to let Mamouli and Annie think Papouli was just sulking, and that he had merely given Dad a suspension, as he sometimes did when the ape got to strutting his stuff too vainly. We weren't about to tell them that Lazarus was off burying Dad. We figured our star would at least show up for the finale, and Bimbo could take Papouli's place on the wire.

With the chimps gone, it was solely up to me to create the original chaos. I couldn't concentrate on creating order at the same time. The dogs kept whining at the door. The cats, who had been giving rides to children for several hours, figured they had done their duty. They prowled around the truck, growling to be fed. Pegasus stood outside, bridled and saddled in bright red but glum as an old dray horse. Polyphemus sat in front of the mirror, in his Abe Lincoln trick hat, with eyes closed, jiggling his temples between thumb and forefinger as he ransacked his brain for some stunt he could pull off to send the crowd home happy.

Then Mamouli appeared in the doorway. She calmly asked us to come outside. She looked surprisingly centered. Scrubbed. Rosy. No longer the giggling hysteric at all, but ready to take command. We gathered — humans and animals — in a circle around her. Our spirits revived as soon as she began to outline the plan for the night. She gave us that warm family thrill again, put us gratefully back in touch with our higher selves. She said that she had caused Papouli a lot of suffering lately, but that she felt it had to be done to restore the balance between them, and once she had assumed her proper role he would see how beautiful things could be between them again. Meanwhile, Papouli himself had always said that the best way to heal a rift among ourselves was to concentrate entirely on healing the audience. We must keep our concentration very strong tonight, she said. We must give our show the same dignity and beauty the legendary monk, Barnaby, did when he juggled for Our Lady. She reminded us repeatedly of our spiritual purpose. We felt wonderful listening to her. Our circle began to glow with confidence. Even the cats pushed through and lay down quietly at Mamouli's feet to listen closely.

She outlined an entirely new show that was to be based in the first half on feats of juggling. Wherever Boomie and Lazarus had gone (we had said they went on a picnic and must have fallen asleep or something), we could include them in our plans at intermission if they returned. Meanwhile, we would skip the opening parade. Instead, she asked me to set up the trick table, with D'Alvini's Magic Portfolio on top. We would open with a spot on Bimbo and Bimba as magicians. They would pull the poodles out of the portfolio, followed by Fetch, our various props, and then Polyphemus and herself carrying a stack of dishes, which she would twirl on a stick, tossing them to me as I stepped out from behind the lightboard and brashly tried to juggle them, breaking them all. To make me seem even more the fool, Annie would enter with three heads of lettuce, and I would announce that she had offered to toss the salad and give me a juggling lesson at the same time. While I set up a table with a bowl, wooden spoons and vinegar and oil, Annie would juggle the lettuces with her trunk — the surprise trick they had been working on — then crush them and drop them in the bowl. I would mix the salad, and, as I tied on a bib and sat down to eat it with great ceremony, she would eat it herself and then appear to eat my bib as well.

We were delighted to learn that Annie knew this trick, and laughed when she showed us the lettuces, sure enough juggling them for us. Mamouli applauded our good cheer. She reminded us that the Latin source word for juggler is *joculator*, which means one who makes a joke, and that she relied on all of us to be very funny that night. Levity would have to be brought to its most sublime peak for the finale she had in mind. The final act would no longer involve Lazarus in a scrape with death. She had us bear in mind that the juggler's three main techniques are gentle ones, representing the raising of earth to sky through the mediating symbol of water — the *fountain*, the *shower* and the *cascade*.

Mamouli had never given the pep talk before. I loved the way she did it. I kept hearing echoes of the Great Grand-Papouli's calm, assured voice as he prepared us to perform our mysteries by instilling us with a sense of awe about ourselves: Mamouli reminded us of our rich tradition, and of how much we owed the greats of the past. Even the original Mrs. Poindexter would be honored among our mystical ancestors tonight, she said, since she had indirectly brought us the one whose life we need no longer fear for, the one we raised from the ground. "My children, as a tribute just this night to the late Mrs. Poindexter," she announced, "we will bring our audience into the show with the circus tea ritual originated by the Great Grand-Papouli's dearest friend, Paul Cinquevaldi." We were all delighted, having secretly missed this ritual, which Papouli had cut from the show several years ago, when it began to trouble his conscience that lumps of sugar were involved.

After she had outlined the flow of our performances, Mamouli led us in the Prayer of St. Francis. I don't think any of us had the least premonition of what she was planning, even when her voice trembled at the last line — "and it is in dying that we are born to eternal life." We took her emotion to be a renewal of that mystical intensity we had expected to regain from the old days, had thought the Greatest Fall on Earth would bring us, though it had failed to do so outside the tent because of Mamouli's dispute with Papouli.

• •

I cut the lights. We entered the tent in the dark. The crowd quieted easily. Everything went exactly as planned. I won't describe each act. The high spots for me were Annie's tossed salad, of course, and the way Jack and Jill leaped out of the water when I belly flopped into their tank, passing over the trapeze with such simple, simultaneous and continuously curved movements that it seemed as if I, standing up to my shoulders in the water with arms outspread, were somehow catching them in my hands and tossing them up again.

In everything we did there was a greater flow than before. The natural transition from conjury to the pure, unfaked art of the juggler, for example, should symbolize increased health; and I thought it worked exceptionally well when Polyphemus produced the oranges from his hat and tossed them to Mamouli, who juggled them before they flew, one at a time, to me and I squeezed them into a glass and drank to the health of the audience.

Mamouli's hardest trick of all dazzled even this old pro. I'd forgotten how subtle it was. Circling the Ring of the Sun on the rump of Pegasus, with a little tea table stacked with cups and saucers, a teapot and a sugar bowl set in the saddle, dressed in the old rag doll housewife costume I thought she'd never wear again, Mamouli had her "afternoon tea." After juggling a cup, saucer, pot of tea and big lump of sugar, she caught the saucer, let the cup settle upon it, caught the laggard sugar lump in the cup, changed these from right hand to left, and casually caught the pot and poured herself some tea, which she sipped with dainty pleasure as she circled the ring atop Pegasus. She then repeated the performance, inviting the audience to tea, while Polyphemus, the twins, and I carried the cups into the stands. Each spectator took a sip of Bob's Special Flowergrass Brew and passed it on until everyone had sipped. A hearty sense of communion had been established by the end of the tea ritual. Everyone was ready to follow the instructions I gave over the mike for Mamouli's first-half finale.

She had borrowed three of Boomie's crescent blades. Polyphemus and the twins let a few men in the audience test and attest to the razor sharpness of the outside edges. One man became so involved that he shaved off his beard in a few fast strokes, and that really got everyone interested. I explained that Mamouli would have to catch the boomerangs on the inside, so that they just touched her palms before she flicked them upward again. I lowered my voice and warned very confidentially that her hands would be sliced right off unless every single person present helped her focus absolute attention on the peak of the arc. I asked the audience to stand. They did so without hesitation.

Infants were lifted up. Children scrambled down to stand in the track area. I explained, in the tone of voice I had heard Papouli use when he mesmerized a crowd, that we were offering a kind of meditation. We were counting upon a perfect psychic connection between audience and performer for the success of Mamouli's act. This was what people expected to hear. It's what had brought them to us from such distant places, and they were more than eager to cooperate. They were exhilarated.

So, you see, I may not have beheld Mamouli walking on air later in the show, but I did help create the conditions for it. As she sent the blades spinning in a slow, rising arc toward the roof of the tent, everyone focused on the peak. I explained that we must in no way strain eyes or ears, or tense our muscles. We must simply fix our relaxed, effortless attention on the top of the rising curve.

When the spinning crescent moons had ceased to rise, the peak fixed at an unmoving point some ten feet from the roof. I brought the lights down slowly. There is a large cardboard crescent moon that we keep tucked up under a canvas flap, tied to a reel of black thread. Sometimes we lower this over the Ring of the Moon, as a symbol of the feminine cradle. I lowered this moon, keeping it in the dark until it was just above the arching blades. Then I cut all the house lights. Mamouli, unseen, stepped back, let the blades drop, and gathered them up.

I stayed at the lightboard while all our performers, including Mamouli, exited quietly. Through the canvas shone the pale light of the real full moon. With our eyes accustomed to the dark, we began to see a sliver of silver, with its horns pointing upward, around which I then tightened a pale blue light and brought it in tighter and tighter, until a circle was formed where Mamouli had fastened our gaze. The old moon in the new moon's arms.

At that moment, I felt a wrench of anguish that Papouli was not with us to see the hypnotic effect Mamouli had left in her wake. Nobody moved. Nobody sat down.

I didn't startle the audience from its rapt state but walked slowly out of the tent. I looked in on the dressing room where everyone was rejoicing at the way we'd pulled it off; then I dashed across the field to see how Papouli was faring, and to let Boomie know it was time to get ready for her act. I was in for quite a shock.

• •

I knocked. No answer. The light was on inside, so I knocked again. "She's coming!" Papouli shouted in a voice I did not like at all. Then Boomie screamed. I kicked in the door. She was standing on the bed against the wall, with a boomerang raised in her hand as a weapon. Papouli lay sprawled out naked in a chair. I won't say what he held in his right hand. But in his left he held what I first took to be some kind of whip. Then I realized it was a large swath of Boomie's hair. His eyes were maniacal.

"Get me out of here," Boomie hissed.

When we were outside, she collapsed in my arms. I carried her to the dressing room. Mamouli didn't say a word. Her face became fiercely confident. She set the example by refusing to be brought down. Using the old trick of shock reversal, she wrapped a blanket around Boomie, took her from me, rocked her and kissed her and said, "Let's do this half for Boomie." It was corny, but it worked. Our spirits perked up again. "Bobby," she said, "I'm putting you in charge. Break them up. Leave it to me and the children to put them back together again." Promising to return as soon as Boomie was cleaned up and put to bed, she carried her off to the Papouli wagon.

Luckily, Lazarus drove up and jumped out of the truck just after that. He asked about Boomie right away. We simply told him that she was exhausted and that Mamouli was looking after her and that he wasn't going to fall from the wire tonight; he could be any kind of clown he pleased. "All you have to do tonight," I said, "is be funny. I want you to lead the way."

Thus challenged, Lazarus was quick to suit up. He

pulled on a candystriped leotard and painted himself a funny face for a change, with a grin that came up to his ears. We went out there and cracked them up with our funniest routines, taking tremendous risks. Lazarus and I fell repeatedly on our backs and on our faces, ending with the one where he falls off a table into my pants, and the poodles jump in after him, and my pants explode, and they all fly out. Christ! Whatever our troubles, the crowd was ready for mayhem, and we let them have it. By the time we had made a total wreck of the arena, everyone had exhausted their laughter and was ready to concentrate again. I dropped the net for the twins' final up-in-smoke routine. The crowd became hushed, expecting something even more spectacular than before. Bimbo and Bimba did not disappoint.

They swung toward each other, smoke pouring from the jets at their waists. Releasing their trapezes at the height of the swing, they slipped right out of the moon-hole at the top of the tent, belly to belly. You could just barely see them through the smoke. They were like vanishing ghosts or spirits. Everybody was in pure awe, including me. I stood there in the Ring of the Moon, gaping upward.

Mamouli, seated on Annie, was already in the center of the Sun Ring before I realized they'd entered the tent. Annie was dressed in her East Indian mirror-glass outfit, saddled with her red, lacquered safari seat. Mamouli was naked to the waist, with a crown of sapphires that sent streaks of blue shooting out all around her head. Between her high, full, swollen breasts, with their marvelously orbed fat red nipples, hung a necklace of pearls that Boomie must have given her from her hoard. She wore a new pair of lavendar tights ruffled with silver below the knee. Barefoot, she stepped out of the saddle and stood in the curve of Annie's trunk, the unmistakable queen mother of the mystical circus. Annie lowered Mamouli to the ground.

As she walked toward the ladder, I walked toward it too. What she had in mind was beginning to dawn on me, and I knew I should do something to stop her. But there was a kind of dazzle to the moment, and the authority was clearly hers. I took hold of the ladder, which was not tied to the ground, as some ladders are, but hung free, and I pulled it to one side.

"What should I announce?" I asked.

She yanked the ladder from my hand and set her foot on the first rung. "Lower me a mike," she said firmly. "I'll do my own announcing."

I seized the ladder again. But how could I struggle with her in front of our public? "Do your job, Bobby," she said. "Give me a spot." A horror welled up in me then. I knew perfectly well what was going to happen, but I have this weakness. Never mind, this is not the place to justify myself. I'm a fool (coward?). I'm too used to taking commands. I ran to the board — ran! And you should never run at a time like that. I ran to the board, cut the lights and followed her up the ladder with the spot.

When she reached the platform, how can I describe my emotion? I wanted to cry out. And yet she looked so beautiful, like one of those elephants you see in the Tibetan *tankas,* a voluptuous symbol of fecundity. My utter despair at what was to come was paralyzed by a great rush of hope. I did my job. That's all I could do. I was helpless to change the course of events. Suddenly Lazarus was beside me.

"What the hell are you doing!"

"I'm lowering a mike," I heard myself say. "Listen."

"You're insane!" Lazarus said. But I hushed him.

"Listen."

"Ladies and gentlemen, boys and girls," Mamouli said in a mellow, deep, elephant voice. "This is the most important night of my life."

"Jesus!" cried Lazarus. He sprinted for the ladder. She saw him coming. She let go of the mike, got down on her knees on the platform, pulled the ladder up out of his reach and hung it on a hook. She stood again, took the mike, and resumed. It was the same speech she had given last time she tried to walk on air. She told of how she had been preparing this act ever since she walked up onto the branch of a tree at age five, how she knew that everyone's life would be changed by what was to come, and how she needed their faith. They were the ones who would keep her in the air. They were the ones who would prevent her from falling. She spoke very slowly, with long pauses during which the listeners became ever quieter and more attentive.

Then I realized that Lazarus was beside me, whispering in my ear. "Cut the mike," he kept saying. I finally got the message and cut it. "Give me a hand mike," he whispered. "Cut all the lights except the spot on Mamouli. Give me sound."

I did so, but before he could speak to the crowd there was an explosion like the crack of a rifle. Mamouli had just unscrewed and released the highwire. It snapped across to the opposite platform, whipped around the pole and slithered across the ground. Lazarus waited until the metal of the pole had stopped singing, then he spoke while I slipped a pink gel into the spot and brought it up brighter on Mamouli. She was crouched up there ready to spring. There was no stopping her now. My stomach was knotted tight. I could hardly breathe. But Lazarus managed to speak calmly enough.

"That's right, good folks," he said. "Tonight we're going to present the Great Mamouli in her new act. Walking on Air! Let's hear it, Robert."

I don't know how I managed a drumroll, but I did.

"Yes, dear friends, because the moon's full tonight and the planets are just where we need them to be, and because you're absolutely without compare the greatest audience we've ever had under our top, our beloved Mamouli, queen of The Great Papouli Circus, has chosen you as the people for whom she will perform a stunt that will raise your consciousness to heights unimaginable and open up possibilities for each and every one of you that you never even dreamed of. But, ah, my friends! If you think such a stunt can be performed by Mamouli alone, let me remind you that she *does* require the assistance of every animal, every bird, every bug and fly, every star that shines through from that hole in the sky. Every performer and every member of the audience gathered here tonight. Your love! Yes, only your intense love beamed toward this wonderful woman you see poised above you . . ."

I can't remember everything Lazarus said. It was a rather flowery speech, praising all Mamouli had done for us through the years, unabashedly eulogizing the sacrifice and compassion of mothers, the need to see them shining down upon us again in their glory. High poetic emotion embarrasses a down-to-earth grunt-of-a-person like me. I would have thought someone would burst out laughing at the tremolo that had come into Lazarus's voice. But they hung on every word. They spontaneously rose to their feet, crossed arms over their chests and held hands. All he had to ask was that they make a sound, any sound. A tremendous humming and babbling of voices filled the tent, rising and falling in closer and closer harmonies until I felt myself being lifted on waves of happiness to the place where Mamouli stood smiling down upon us, hands pressed together at her breast. Among the voices was the giddy, tinkling, distant watermusic of notes being struck on glass bells. Mamouli stepped onto the air.

For an instant she floated. She seemed to stand on the waves we had lifted to support her. Then she fell. But for the others it was just a deep trough she fell into between the waves, an oceanic abyss out of which she was lifted back up to an even higher wave. They saw her spring out of her body and ride, as if on the crest of their voices, standing at her full majestic height, in a curve around the Ring of the Sun, then across to the Ring of the Moon, where she stopped, appearing to stand upon that crescent sliver of a new moon. And then, as if gathering all the energy from the full moon that shone directly down upon the tent, she beamed a blue light from her body, a pale blue light down upon the Circle of the Sun.

People saw her standing on air all night, and all the next day and the next night, and some people see her standing there still. Soon they were swarming down from the stands to dance in the pole of blue light. But I was gone by then, and I saw none of that. What I saw was that she fell hard to the ground and stayed there.

I don't wish to destroy an illusion. I don't even say it was an illusion. Maybe the illusion was only mine, and it seems petty to tell my point of view. But this is *my* notebook, after all.

I don't blame Annie in the least for what happened. I can imagine exactly what went through her head. As Mamouli stepped from the platform and floated for an instant, Annie thought of Papouli, how he absolutely must see this or he would go on refusing to believe. Another possibility is that she simply panicked, realizing that Papouli alone could save the one she loved. All I know is that Annie sped out of the tent to fetch Papouli. I believe it must have been her giant compassion, her elephantine faith, that kept Mamouli briefly aloft, because the instant she was out of sight Mamouli fell.

I rushed to Mamouli's side. I saw that she was dying. That's all I'll say. If something else occurred, I wish to God I'd seen it. How was I to look up at a time like that?

• •

Whatever Annie managed to communicate to Papouli, he came to his senses fast. He was out of the wagon before he even thought to put on his clothes. The rest I must tell from hearsay. I've heard enough, that's for sure. Our circus family and the crowd of that night — they're all great friends now. Everyone hangs about the grounds grinning with lustrous eyes.

They say that when Papouli stumbled into the tent, he

found himself quickly enclosed in a circle around the central circle of the Sun Ring. Hands reached out and drew him in. He was caught up and lifted by the rise and fall of voices. It was a celestial music that startled him out of his misery. He looked up to where the eyes of all the crowd were fixed, and there stood his Mamouli. She spread her arms for him and folded them and spread them again, as if she were flying, and some say that she laughed before she resumed her original pose. The twins saw it, the animals saw it, even Polyphemus stood in the circle and sang as he gazed. Lazarus must have seen it, because otherwise I don't think he would have been so quick to forgive Papouli for what he had done to Boomie. He has refused to hold any grudge against him to this day, though Boomie keeps her distance from our dazzled chieftain — not that he would notice her if she passed right next to him, his eyes remain so fixed upon the sky.

I took Mamouli to the hospital. I held her in the ambulance while the last rattle of breath escaped her throat. I signed the death papers. I stayed in town the next day to take care of the funeral. When I returned, I was shocked and hurt and confused to find that everyone was still milling about in a state of rapture. It would have been useless to try to convince anyone inside or outside the family, except Boomie, to attend the burial. So we went alone. I said a few words as the casket was lowered. Boomie knelt and wept. I put my hand on her head and loved her more than ever. We drove home in silence. She went to her wagon and I went to mine.

Yes, I'm over it now; but for many days I deeply resented the fact that everyone else was going around looking happy and excited, as if they wouldn't have missed Mamouli's death for anything on earth. As if there were no death. As if, since she walked on air, death was just a joke.

37

Tomorrow I'll set forth on Boomie's flying motorcycle, dressed in a flashy spangled jacket, my hair expensively groomed and feathered. I'll be the barker for the twins' new circus. The Electric Medicine Show!

We'll perform inside a solar-heated glass dome with panels that swing open to let the birds fly in. The twins will swoop in on hang gliders, with the flock that Boomie left behind. She's married to Lazarus now, and they're off raising temples. I'm glad she put away her blades. I wish I could find a woman like Boomie. Maybe I will, now that she's not around for me to worry about. Her happiness has released something in me and given me a new kind of nerve. I never would have dared burn down the tent before.

Yep, Bob the mad arsonist gave it the torch. I'd had enough of all those pilgrims swarming about. They're searching elsewhere for their miracles now. The spiritual aloofness they generated cut me off emotionally from the rest of the circus body for quite some time. That's no problem any more. I hold no grudges. I'll be glad to join the twins. They can dress me up like Paul Revere, and I'll fly into town on the back of Pegasus before every show crying, "The new age is coming! The new age is coming!" I'll gallop through the streets with their good-news journal in my saddle bags and deliver like I did when I was a boy. Back on the circus grounds, I'll stand on a platform in a suit of lights, in front of the ticket booth, summoning the crowd, and I won't be conning them either. It's the circus we've always needed, with healers and mystical mechanics. We'll be teaching herbal medicine, massage, magic, meditation through juggling and wirewalking, levitation, acupuncture, chanting and dervish dancing. The twins have designed and built the rides not to scare you or to make you scream but to center you, to make you cry out in wonder. What we want to bring our audience, say Bimbo and Bimba, is pure *ekstasis,* the leap out of oneself into the light.

This is being written on the steps of the wagon I'll abandon tomorrow along with the rest of the wagons and the baggage of the defunct Great Papouli Circus. I think of this as having been our blue and rose period, the age when we were still standing wanly in a field, balancing on a ball; or in a dressing room, dreaming before the mirror of becoming a dove. Picasso was our chronicler. For what's coming, I think we'll need someone humble enough to learn the mystical lesson of the untormented beast left free to roam untrained in the Great Garden; someone on the order of William Blake.

I look over at that cute little outhouse across the field,

with the moon on the side like a fading image of one of Boomie's boomerangs. The privy was waiting for us when we arrived at this site last year. My original plan was to try to publish my notebooks, complete with my own illustrations, then send them as a surprise to Papouli. But he doesn't want to remember what happened on the ground. He's keeping his image of Mamouli up in the air, juggling the sun and moon and stars, you might say. Who knows but what Papouli is still seeing some kind of vision of the mother within the high-peaked mountain? But here I am, a disbeliever, giving over to an ever more extravagant fantasy of what it must be like for those who have experienced her transfiguration.

Down, Bob. Down to earth where you belong.

The gypsies who camped here before us left a stack of astrology magazines in the privy. It occurred to me the other day just to skip the whole publication circuit and take my notebook over there and leave it with the magazines, for Polyphemus to browse through and then use as he deems fit. An appropriate last gesture by the man in charge of wiping up.

Polyphemus is going to hang around. He says there's no place he'd rather be than where he happens to find himself. I see him across the way under his canvas awning. He'll be the only performer left. He already has his new act going. The hammock he's working on is strung between two poles like a badminton net. His huge hands send the shuttle deftly flying. He has an audience seated out there in folding chairs — children and adults. They come to watch him or to play with the poodles. The poodles are all over the place now. They look like a flock of sheep, especially when they're corralled at shearing time. Something about the death of a mother figure arouses a tremendous urge to reproduce. Once Fetch was gone, a pack of male dogs showed up and didn't leave until every one of my poodles had come into heat and been ravished. After that, I don't know, I just didn't feel like sleeping with them any more. Go ahead and laugh. I felt betrayed — not me, you understand, but the spirit of Fetch in me. My best friend was barking at those surly curs the whole time, barking from inside me. At least the poodle strain dominated. It makes an excellent yarn.

Polyphemus cards the poodle hair and spins it. He gathers berries, roots and flowers, and boils the dye in giant cauldrons. He puts on quite a show, though he hardly talks at all any more. In fact, he pays his audience no heed except when a hammock's finished. Then he sells it and starts on another. The shuttle fish darts through a sea of soft colors. Look. He's cutting one down. A woman's right there to hand him his price. She rolls it under her arm and hurries to her car to race on home. What clowns we are. She's going to string it up between two trees just as fast as she can, climb into that soft poodle hair, fold herself into a cocoon and sleep until she emerges a butterfly. The urge to fly with wings of our own possesses more of us every day. I feel certain that flights of angels — the flying creatures our dolphins used to speak of, who flit through space from star to star — are on their way to guide us. Though Mamouli had to meet them on the other side, I don't think we'll even have to wait for death, if we just keep up the heart-and-soul cry of imagination.

But as for me, when everyone flies off I'd like to stay behind and disguise myself, perhaps as a four-legged creature, and watch the earth become a garden again. Pardon me, Mamouli, but I don't think the earth is dying. It's only changing. What's dying is the conquering spirit of man over nature — and just in the nick of time. Let the new human being arise. The sooner the better. Aren't we all at the end of our patience from worrying about cancer and the like because we ourselves have become the cancers of this earth? We'll get well just as quickly as we help the earth get well. That seems obvious even to a clod like me.

If we marveled once that we tamed the beast and put him through his tricks, let's marvel now without defiance. Then gravity may change to levity. The trick's in such a simple psychic change. I learned it from the Japanese clown, Natoni. He used to draw two circles on a piece of paper while we were fooling around in the dressing room waiting to go on. The circles appeared to have the same weight, of course; but when he drew the stem of an apple atop one and the string of a kite under the other, the one with the string suddenly seemed incredibly lighter. In those days I was one of those clowns who mixed with the audience, selling exactly that — apples and balloons; and I thought a lot about this trick of Natoni's. The apple needs the stem to say up in the tree. The balloon needs the string to stay down in the little kid's fist. Most kids cry when their balloon flies off. But the image I love best is of that special child who stands looking up, wide-eyed, biting into his apple while he watches the balloon he purposely let go of rise to the roof of the tent. Ach! I'm a clown. I don't know what it all means. All I know is, I don't really have anything against Newton. I like my gravity just fine, too. I even like the weight of this notebook, as I prepare to lay it in my left hand and kiss it goodbye.

I'm going over to see if I can get at least a small rise out of Polyphemus. It would be nice for him to find one of his brilliant thoughts in my very last entry.

38

"WHAT'S ON YOUR MIND?" said I to the giant, in a perfectly cheerful, comradely way, I assure you.

He stopped his weaving and looked at me with exasperation. "Nothing. Nothing was on my mind until you interrupted."

"Well, I'm sorry," I said. "I only wanted to say goodbye. It was thoughtless of me." I looked at the audience seated in their tin chairs watching. "Excuse me, folks." Once again I turned to leave, wondering why I ever bothered to approach him any more.

He caught me by the back of the neck, turned me around, lifted me up and gazed at me with curiosity. "Poor Robert, you'll have to learn to think before you can arrive at thoughtlessness."

He gave me a warm, heartfelt hug, Polyphemus did, and awkward as I felt up there with my chin hooked on his shoulder, smouldering as I was from that tone of intellectual haughtiness I so detest, I nevertheless was deeply moved. I didn't know Polyphemus had that much affection in him. He held me against his chest and squeezed me hard. "Goodbye, Robert," he whispered. "Let's say farewell now and have done with it. No tears, please." He set me down, turned me around and patted me on the behind.

So much for a wise word from Polyphemus. He's out of it. I hope I never blow a fuse on thought. There's still so much to figure out. I don't think I'm such a bad thinker, and I'm going to get better, but not so good that I want to quit for the sake of my enlightenment. I like mulling things over. For example: Would you like to hear Bob the Grip's Chimpanzic Theory of Evolution? It celebrates the jellyfish and suchlike as advanced forms of life, following through on the notion that thought is an early stage of evolution that precedes the rhythmic perfection of purely instinctual being. Deep, what? We clowns like to take ourselves seriously. That's how we make fun of ourselves. How can you overlook what you're undergoing without losing the fun of finding yourself in the middle of it? Ho Ho. Ach! Poly's right. I should calm my confused mind, let our story figure itself out. I'll just end by telling you what happened to the others; I'll tie a few strings, tuck in loose ends and be off.

• •

I took Jack and Jill to the coast of California and dumped them into the sea. Such gladness as they leaped over the waves, tail-walking into the brightness of the horizon. What fools we were ever to keep them in a tank. They, who have always loved to put on a much vaster show.

I biked into town recently to check the mail at general delivery. There was a letter with a nifty stamp on it from Africa, and a photo of a lioness chasing an antelope while a lion surrounded by cubs watches lazily from under a tree.

Sir or Ms.:

A rather old lion appeared in our camp who behaves quite tamely. Though he appears morose and somewhat disoriented, he is in good health. A tab on his ear gives his address as The Great Papouli Circus, so we have traced your location and notify you herewith that we would dearly like to make a pet of the old gentleman, but that if you want him back we must ask you to pay for packing and delivery.

Yours truly,

George and Dorothy Mayer
Senior Wardens
Poets and Painters Wildlife Refuge
Olatunde, Nigeria

I replied with a request that Calypso be shipped air freight C.O.D., as per my arrangements, to the address of Mr. and Mrs. Solomon in Orlando, Florida. I'm sure the Solomons will be glad to have Calypso around. They could fit him into their act.

The Solomons are doing quite well these days. They're living in semi-retirement in a trailer camp beside an orchard, where they put on an occasional show but mostly just hang out with the makers of pure nonsense upon whom they have placed their hopes. They play shuffleboard, watch TV and go to the track to bet on the trotters.

Annie? There is a canyon not far from here where the muddy gray boulders below the cliff resemble a procession of elephants. After Mamouli fell, Annie ran away. But I was up in that canyon for a swim one afternoon when I saw the boulders begin to move. I like to think that Annie was taking them for a slow stroll. Elephants know that even the rocks breathe. And she, with her giant compassion, must have wanted to show them the beauty of the view just around the bend, looking down past the railroad track to the river.

I have also heard that clouds like to linger over clods freshly turned by the plow of a reverent farmer. Perhaps they're attracted to certain kinds of rocks, too. With a little guidance from an elephant, the clouds might very well want to roll along over the boulders, awakening their somnolent dreams of rising from the earth.

Fetch died of sorrow, as dogs do, and is off in heaven, perhaps chasing a stick for Mamouli. I was reminded by him how all creatures need to die at dusk, with their muzzles pointed directly at the setting sun. They like to die near water, under a tree, covered with leaves, with a fire nearby; and they like to have a guardian — not to trouble them with anxiety about death but to protect them from intrusion. Death, the most sublime creative act (I have come to see this with Mamouli's death), should never be interrupted.

When Fetch died, a pale glow hovered around his body for an hour or so. After the glow was gone, we dug him a grave and buried him. He reminded us what a beautiful, tender and attentive act death can be when carried off with devotion. If I had known that Mamouli was choosing to die, perhaps I could have regarded her final performance that way.

From the night she walked on air perhaps to this moment, Papouli has not looked at the ground, for fear of what he might see. Refusing to accept Mamouli's death, he held fast to the vision. But his heart was broken at the same time. Thus does one part of us know what another part denies.

I know what a broken heart is, since Boomie once broke mine. Heartbreak is no mere metaphor. It is a wrenchingly painful event, worse by far than a broken leg or even a broken skull. But the heart mends. I'm sure Papouli's okay now. I wonder if he does look down to earth again.

They say there are caves on the island where he went to spend his last days. You have to climb down a cliff to reach one, and if you sit at its lip you can see the roiling torrent below. I wonder if Papouli watches the water or if he still plays the compleat idiot, following the dance of the one he loves, among the birds and clouds and stars.

If he hadn't gone into seclusion, people would have made a saint of him. A man who walks about with face upraised can deceive people. In truth, he was but a bewildered man whose goodness was marred by a tragedy our age is finally coming to terms with. Papouli's faith in woman could never equal the faith he had in man. Adoration, I regret to say, is no substitute. This is only my humble view, but I don't think we can compensate for our misbehavior on earth with visions of miraculous transcendence.

Papouli used to speak frequently about the day he'd

set forth for his island. It never seemed to occur to him, let alone worry him, that Mamouli would suffer from his absence. My, but he did suffer, when it turned out to be she who set forth. A vision is a poor substitute for flesh and blood. I finally had my own vision of Mamouli, despite my reluctance.

I had walked out to the country to look for Papouli. There he was, up on a rise, his hair, which had turned suddenly white, blowing in the wind. He was leaning back, hands in pockets, gazing as usual at the sky. It being suppertime, I was going up to him to lead him back to camp when right there in a tree her face appeared.

It's hard to remember whether I saw the whole body or not. All I remember is the radiant face of a young girl, fresh with the excitement of some fantastic adventure she was about to embark on. I have seen similar faces in the windows of buses, when parents send their children off to perform together in some distant city.

Mamouli was off to show an audience of stars that she could walk in space. She was off to lift consciousness to the giddy heights that virgin life aims for in its freshest confidence. She assured us that she was very happy, having joined another circus of marvelous entertainers who were awaiting her up there just ahead. She had to hurry on. She just wanted us to know that we needn't grieve for her any more. We could go on celebrating our lives, start a new and better circus of our own.

I took Papouli's big head in my hands and pressed my cheek against his. "Did you see her?" I asked him. "Did you hear?"

It was good finally to feel his chest heave. He didn't

answer. He just began to sob, and he sobbed on and on while I stood there holding him long into the night. We were standing, I realized, on the very hill where he had fought it out with his own shadow and had struck it dead.

As for Lazarus? He's back being buried in the ground. With Boomie's help he's gone worldwide. She attracts people to his grave by the thousands, the way she dances and sings and shakes her tambourine as she collects the money. She's made him a legend. According to the radio, he's been in the ground beside the Jordan River for going on forty days. This is the great test of his career (aren't they all?). Nobody would think to raise him prematurely. The Great Lazarus has achieved his myth. Either love raises him up, or he dies.

Whether this is the truth or the legend Boomie weaves into her songs (you can buy them at your record store), they say he raised a palace in Poland fit for a pope. He raised a barn in India where holy cows stand in stained-glass niches, with candlelit images of Krishna fluting, while maids come to milk them on their wedding day. He raised a thunder lodge in Mongolia, a chapel in southern France, the sanctuary of an occult Nile priestess in Alexandria, and a mosque in Jerusalem.

Now he's raising a great temple to be built by the people of his own ancestral nation, a temple to elevate the consciousness of all humankind. I have a bottle of sacramental wine here, which Boomie stole that day she went to get the holy water we sprinkled on Mamouli's platform. Boomie had wanted us to drink of it, each lifting our glass to the Queen of Heaven before Mamouli stepped into the air. Papouli said it was bad luck to do ritual with stolen goods, but I think Boomie had the right idea, and I saved the bottle. It's never too late. I hear the gods laughing. Do it, they say. Life is for life.

So, on this last day, I set glasses before me for each member of our mystical body. A glass for Lazarus (*L'chaim!*). A glass for Polyphemus. A glass for Bimbo and Bimba. A glass for Mamouli. A glass for Papouli. A glass for Boomie. A hearty wine, yes, fit to lift the spirits. I have drunk me all of it and broken the glasses against the stove.

Now, a last glass from the bottom for us, my sisters and brothers.